PROUD TO BE A HINDU

Vijay Bhatnagar

गरुड

Published by
Garuda Prakashan Private Limited
Gurugram, Bharat

www.garudalife.in

First published in Bharat 2025

ISBN: 978-81-994386-0-6

Printed in Bharat

Contents

Acknowledgements

The author gratefully acknowledges the editorial team of Garuda Prakashan for their useful suggestions for improvements to the original draft of the manuscript. The author also acknowledges the contributions of his wife Pushpa and son Gaurav by way of suggestions and ideas during the writing of this book, and for their patient proof reading of several drafts to make the final manuscript as error free as possible.

Preface

One of the enduring paradoxes post the Partition of India is this: After six centuries of oppressive Muslim rule and decades of Hindu-Muslim conflict leading to division of the motherland, the natural corollary would have been Hindu consolidation as a bulwark against history repeating itself. However, nothing of the sort happened. Despite losing a substantial portion of their ancient motherland in the Partition, Hindus moved on as if nothing extraordinary had occurred. Why? Several reasons may help explain this collective amnesia:

1. Effect of Slavery Itself

There is a term *Stockholm Syndrome* which is used to describe a psychological condition in which a captive develops a grudging admiration for their captor. At its core, it reflects a dynamic where the weak stand in awe of the powerful. What holds true for individuals can also apply to entire societies. After enduring six centuries of Muslim rule, followed by two centuries of British domination, it is hardly surprising that Hindu society internalized a deep sense of inferiority and powerlessness vis-à-vis the 'other.'

2. Self-Doubt About the Glory of Our Ancient Culture, Civilization, and Religion

Most Hindus came to resemble the descendants of a once-great lineage, now fallen on hard times. There lingered a vague but persistent awareness that they hailed from an ancient civilization with a luminous past. Yet, the relentless traumas of the preceding 800 years had sown deep seeds of self-doubt: If we were truly so great, why were we unable to defend ourselves against foreign invaders? Some of our political leaders contributed to this sense of self doubt in no small measure. Chief among them was India's first Prime Minister, Jawaharlal Nehru, who made no secret of his disdain for what he dismissively termed 'Hindu revivalism.' Curiously, this aversion was never directed at the revivalism of other faiths. His selective secularism only deepened the disconnect between a newly independent nation and its civilizational roots.

3. Pseudo Secularism

After the Partition of India, on clear communal lines and creation of a separate state for Muslims namely Pakistan, what was left should logically have been organised as a Hindu state, not in the sense of a theocratic state but as an assertion of the fact that vast majority of its citizens were Hindus with its ancient civilization dating back to over 5000 years. In keeping with its motto of *Sarva Dharma Sambhav* (equal respect for all religions), adherents of all other religions would have had equal rights and respect in such a state. If some political leaders had aversion to the word 'Hindu' the least they could have done was to have strived for a genuinely secular state in which all citizens irrespective of their religion would have equal rights. Instead, what they did was i) incorporated articles in the constitution granting special rights to the so-called minorities, thus negating the fundamental principle of true secularism and ii) mollycoddled and appeased Muslims for their votes. This led to consolidation of Muslims as a vote bank. Hindus being divided on the basis of castes, languages, regions and so forth, formula for power was set: divide Hindus on the basis of caste, language etc and appease Muslims for their vote bank. Ironically, they did it in the garb of secularism.

4. Downplaying the Glory of Hindu culture and civilization

Glorifying Hindu culture and civilization was branded as 'communal.' Ideally, school children should have been taught about Bharatvarsh's ancient Hindu culture and civilization - inspirational stories from scriptures, great achievements in various fields such as arts, architecture, ethics, administration, law, message of *Gita* and about great warriors from history. But it was not allowed to be done because doing so would have upset the vote banks. The result is telling: ask the average person to name an architectural marvel of Bharatvarsha, and the answer will almost inevitably be the Taj Mahal—not Ajanta or Ellora. This brand of 'secularism,' as practiced in Bharatvarsha, has inflicted immense damage on the Hindu cause—most gravely, on the community's self-esteem and self-confidence.

This book is a humble attempt by the author to highlight some of the above-mentioned issues, with a view to awaken the Hindus from the slumber and proclaim to the world once again with pride that WE ARE PROUD TO BE HINDUS.

Chapter-1

Sanatan Civilization and Religion

Sanatan civilization is the only ancient civilization in continuous existence for at least 5000 years. Sanatan is the mother of what we today call the Hindu religion. While the terms Sanatan, Hindu religion, and Dharma are often used interchangeably, they are not identical. It is important to first distinguish between Sanatan civilization, the Hindu religion, and Dharma.

Sanatan Civilization

Some fundamental principles/beliefs form the bedrock of every civilisation. These principles/beliefs are eternal (*shashvat*) and people belonging to the civilization, by and large, uphold them. Some of the fundamental principles/beliefs of Sanatan are:

1. The universe is created by an all-powerful entity (whom we call *Ishwar* or God) who runs and sustains it and annihilates it in due course.

2. God is omnipresent i.e. God does not have a specific place of residence. He is present everywhere and in everything (living and non-living), throughout the universe.

3. Every living being has a divine element which we call *Atma* (or soul). A living being is alive so long as the *Atma* resides in its physical body. As the living being dies, the *Atma* leaves its body and enters another physical body. This phenomena of *Atma* leaving one body and entering another and then another can be called the cycle of birth, death and rebirth. There are innumerable kinds of living being, each one of these kinds is known as a *Yoni*. In the hierarchy of *Yonis*, human *Yoni* is the highest. After undergoing births in numerous lower *Yonis*, the human *Yoni* is achieved and once human *Yoni* is achieved, the *Atma* does not go back to a lower *Yoni*.

4. In the human *Yoni*, where the *Atma* will be reborn - whether the life in the next birth will be happy or miserable, depends upon the nature of deeds in the present birth. Good deeds or bad deeds in the present birth result in a good life or miserable in the next birth. In other words, good or bad experiences in the present birth are the result of the nature of deeds (good or bad) done in the previous birth. This is in consonance with the principle laid down by Lord Krishna in Gita – Perform *karma* (deeds, duties) well without worrying about the outcome, implying that good deeds will lead to good outcome. Therefore, worrying about the result is pointless.

5. Ultimate objective of every human being (*Atma)* is *Moksh* – release from the cycle of birth and rebirth and permanent union with *Paramatma* (God).

6. There is only one omnipresent God, but people perceive Him differently, as per their own faith and belief [*Ekam Sat Vipra Bahudha Vadanti* (*Rig Veda*) – There is only one truth (God), wise perceive Him differently].

7. Upanishads proclaim - *Vasudhaiva Kutumbakam* (meaning *Vasudha* = Earth/World, *iva* = Like, *Kutumbakam* = Extended family) - The world is a unified, interconnected and interdependent entity, just like a family. In a family, the members are interdependent; they complement and supplement each other. Similarly, different constituents of the world such as humans, earth (plains, mountains, deserts), sky (air), water bodies (rivers, lakes, oceans), animal kingdom, vegetation etc. form a unified and integrated system. It emphasises the need for harmony not just among the human beings inhabiting the mother earth, but also that of human beings with other elements of nature. Any adverse impact on any one constituent is bound to impact other constituents similarly. *

* Truth of this dictum is being realised by the world in the form of environmental degradation, global warming, extreme natural events such as rains, floods,

draughts, cyclones etc., fast melting of glaciers, earthquakes etc.

Dharma

Hindus use the term '*Dharma*' to describe the duties relating to different roles people play in society such as *Pati dharma* (Husband's duty), *Patni dharma* (Wife's duty), *Putra dharma* (Son's duty) and *Raj dharma* (Ruler's duty). In *Sanatan* tradition, utmost emphasis is laid upon everybody doing one's duty towards other family members, society, country etc. In fact, the rights and duties for different roles are well laid down in scriptures. Hence, use of the word '*Dharma*' to represent Hindu religion in the sense we use it to describe other religions (say Islam or Christianity) is not correct. For Hindu religion (worship of God, rituals etc) we can use the term *Puja padhyati* (way of worship). In day-to-day parlance when we use the term *Hindu Dharma*, it encompasses *Sanatan*, duties (of a Hindu) and the method of worship, rituals etc.

Ways of Worship (*Puja Padhati*)

For most other religions, the ways of worship and rituals are prescribed in their respective religious texts (for example The *Quran*, *Hadith* and similar texts for Muslims). These edicts are inviolable to the extent that any deviation is considered blasphemous and invites severe punishment. Hindu religion is different in this respect. There are no specified rituals to be mandatorily followed by every Hindu. Every Hindu is free to choose or devise their own methodology for worship. They are even free to perceive the form of God (*sakar brahm*) or may worship a formless God (*nirakar*). This is a unique freedom enjoyed by Hindus alone.

Sanatan/Hindu Religion and Concept of God

As stated earlier, every Hindu is free to perceive the nature and form of God to worship. This unique freedom has led to the conception of innumerable forms of God (*Devi/Devatas*). In the most ancient texts of Hindus viz. the Vedas, God has been perceived as all powerful, all pervasive, implying a formless God. Further, Vedas and Upanishads generally talk of one God as evident from the following *shloka* from Chandogya Upanishad:

Ekameva Advitiyam Brahma – There is Brahma (God) alone, the one without a second.

Question arises, if God is one then who are Brahma, Vishnu and Mahesh (Siva). Further, how and why so many *Devis/Devatas* were conceived? Some obvious reasons for the above are as follows:

1. Mere fact that the universe exists, functions in a smooth and orderly manner and every object in the universe earthly or celestial must perish in due course, would raise the following questions:
   i) Who created it? Afterall, every creation must have a **Creator**.

ii) No system functions in an orderly manner on its own. So, who sustains universe's orderly functioning i.e. who is the **Sustainer**?

iii) Who destroys what has been created i.e. who is the **Destroyer**?

Ancient thinkers (*Rishis)* would have philosophised about existence of one superior being (God) who had to have limitless powers (omnipotent) and had to be all pervasive (omnipresent) to create, sustain and destroy a creation as vast as the universe. For the benefit of the layman, who needs physical symbols to understand complex phenomena, the *Rishis* perceived God's three physical forms of Brahma (the Creator), Vishnu (the Sustainer) and Shiva (the Destroyer) to represent three broad functions of one (and only one) supreme being.

2. As discussed above, Hindus essentially believe in existence of one God who manifests as the Creator (Brahma), the Sustainer (Vishnu) and the Destroyer (Shiva). Then who are various *Devatas* mentioned in scriptures?

God's power is not revealed only at the scale of the universe; it surrounds us in every moment of daily life. The Sun gifting us light and warmth, clouds releasing lifegiving rain, the gentle flow of air, rivers quenching our thirst, trees and plants bearing fruits and grains—all are manifestations of the divine, sustaining life in countless ways. In Sanatan tradition, these aspects of

God's power have been conceived in physical form as *Devatas* (the divine being, boon giver) - Indra (rain), Varun (ocean), Agni (fire), Prithvi (earth), Surya (sun), Chandrama (moon), Vat-Vriksh (banyan tree), Tulsi (holy basil), Ganga (river), Yamuna (river), Kailash (mountain) etc. Hindus worship *Devatas* as the physical manifestation of God. Through the worship of *Devatas*, Hindus express their gratitude to God for providing the life sustaining boons and a prayer for His continued blessings.

Who Is a Hindu?

Who is a Hindu? Anyone born as a Hindu is a Hindu. For being a Hindu is it obligatory to follow a specified way of life, way of worship and/or rituals? Is it mandatory to believe and have faith in one or more of the *Devis* and *Devatas*? Is it obligatory for a Hindu to visit temple regularly? Answer to all these posers is– no, for being a Hindu none of these is mandatory. A Hindu is free to adopt any or all the above-mentioned practices or none and this is one of the biggest strengths of Sanatan/Hindu religion. A Hindu enjoys the freedom to even challenge the fundamental precepts of Sanatan and propose new ones based upon one's own understanding and wisdom. Debate (*vaad-prativaad*) has been an integral part of the Sanatan tradition. Sanatan does not seek to declare any principle(s) as ultimate and impose them on all Hindus; rather search for truth (*satya*) and knowledge (*gyan*) are considered as a never ending, timeless process. In ancient times, it was a common practice to conduct debating assemblies (*vaad-prativaad goshthi*) in which scholars would debate on issues such as nature of God, religion, philosophy, public policy, morality etc. Purpose of these assemblies was to advance the frontiers of knowledge through free exchange of ideas. Female scholars (*vidushiyan*) used to freely participate in these assemblies. Gargi, Maitreyi, Yaami, Lopamudra, Vishwavara were some of such female scholars.

Very fact that Buddhism and Jainism (and later Sikhism) branched out of Hindu Religion and prospered is a mark of the freedom of thought available to Hindus. On the other hand, there were *Charvaaks* who did not believe in the existence of God. They lead an unrestrained lifestyle. They believed in the present life being the only life and that it should be fully enjoyed, without restraint and consideration of *paap* (sin) or *punya* (virtue). In a way, all that *Charvaaks* believed in was antithesis of the fundamental principles of Sanatan, yet they were considered as part of the Hindu society. Such has been the level of freedom of thought and belief available to Hindus since ancient times.

How, then, do we define the Hindu religion? To answer this, we must first establish what 'religion' itself means. For clarity, we can examine the nature of the world's two largest religions, Islam and Christianity, as reference points. Some of the characteristics common to these religions are:

1. Both were established by their respective prophets.
2. Fundamental tenets of both the religions are specified in their respective holy books (Quran for Muslims and Bible for Christians). Further, anything and everything written in these holy books are considered by the respective adherents as final and inviolable truths. So much so that, in case of Islam, any statement in contradiction or any action in violation to Quran is considered as blasphemous and invites severe punishment.
3. For adherents of both religions, rituals are well laid down and are to be followed mandatorily.
4. Each one proclaims itself as the only true religion and exhorts others to convert to theirs.

Comparing the Hindu religion with Islam and Christianity, we find that it is totally opposite to these two. It has not been established by a prophet, rather it is the essence of the principles of Sanatan as propounded by sages and seers (*rishi, munies*) over thousands of years. Unlike Islam and Christianity, there is no one holy book to guide Hindus. There are various texts created by sages from time to time, such as *Vedas* (4), *Puranas* (18), *Upanishads, Ramayana,* and *Mahabharat.* There is no single code of conduct or set of rituals which are to be mandatorily adhered to by every Hindu. There are specified rituals for special occasions such as birth, death, marriage etc. However, in day-to-day life, every Hindu is free to follow (or not to follow) any religious routine/rituals as per one's faith and belief. Lastly, Sanatan/Hindu religion does not claim itself to be superior to other religions. Rather, it proclaims '*Sarva Dharm Sambhav*' that is 'All Religions are to be respected equally'.

As against compulsory religious practices and rituals for Muslims (and to some extent for Christians as well), for Hindus, more emphasis is laid upon fulfilling one's duties (*dharma*) and adherence to a virtuous code of conduct in day to day living. In Hindu scriptures most recurrent themes are:

i) Adherence to truth under all circumstances [*satyam eva jayate* (*Mundaka Upanishad*) - Truth indeed prevails]

ii) Performing one's duty at any cost [*karmanye va adhikaraste, ma phaleshu kadachana* (*Bhagvat Gita*) - Performing your duty is within your powers, not its outcome or perform your duty irrespective of the outcome.]

iii) Acquisition of knowledge [*na choraharyam, na cha rajharyam, na bhratribhajyam, na cha bharkari, vyaya krite vardham aiv nityam, vidyadhanam sarva dhan pradhanam* - It can't be stolen by thieves, nor can it be taken away by the king. It can't be divided among brothers. It does not have weight (hence easy to carry). It keeps growing with regular use. Hence, wealth of knowledge is the most superior wealth of all.]

iv) Humility [*namanti phalino vriksha, namanti gudino jana, shushka kashthashcha murkhashcha na namanti kadachana* - Branches of fruits laden tree bend downwards just as highly cultivated people bow down out of humility. The unwise, however, are like the branches of a dry tree, which does not bend (hence is prone to break.]

v) Good character [*videsheshu dhanam vidya. vyasneshu dhanam mati. parloke dhanam dharma. sheelam sarvatra vaye dhanam* - Knowledge is wealth in a foreign land. Intelligence is wealth in adverse times. In the afterword one's good deeds are the wealth. However, good character is wealth everywhere and all times.]

And so forth.

The heroes and role models looked up to by the people belonging to a religion or civilization reveal much about its fundamental values. Apart from Shri Ram and Shri Krishna, revered by Hindus as divine incarnations, there are numerous other exemplary figures from epics, scriptures, and history who serve as role models. These include Bhishma, Vidura, Yudhishthira, Arjuna, Gautama Buddha, Mahavira,

Raja Harishchandra, Rishi Dadhichi, and countless sages (rishis and munis). Each one of them represents one or more of the above-mentioned virtues held as ideals by Hindus through the ages.

So, who is a Hindu? Apart from a born Hindu, anyone who has a sense of belonging to the ancient Sanatan civilization, takes pride in it and believes in the above-mentioned set of principles and values as the guiding light in day-to-day living is a Hindu.

Chapter-2

Hindu Culture & Civilization

In the previous chapter we had discussed the basic aspects of Sanatan and nature of Hindu religion. The Hindu civilization, with an unbroken legacy spanning over 5,000 years, possesses countless other glorious facets that deserve exploration. Here, we will examine some of them.

Architecture/Sculpture

Sarnath, Sanchi (Stupa), Konark (Sun Temple), Nalanda University, Ajanta (with its exquisite paintings adorning the walls and ceilings of rockcut caves), Ellora (especially the aweinspiring monolithic Kailashnath Temple carved toptobottom from a single rock), Mahabalipuram, Khajuraho, and the grand temples of South India—such as the Meenakshi Amman Temple (Madurai), Brihadeeswara Temple (Thanjavur), Padmanabhaswamy Temple (Thiruvananthapuram), Ramanathaswamy Temple (Rameshwaram), Virupaksha Temple (Hampi), and Venkateswara Temple (Tirupati)—stand as magnificent testaments to Hindu achievement in architecture and sculpture. For our present purpose, it will suffice to examine just one example in greater detail to illustrate the glorious heights reached by Hindus in the realms of art, architecture, and sculpture: the caves of Ajanta and Ellora.

Before we proceed further, it is necessary to clear a prevalent misconception (incidental or spread deliberately) that the descriptions of grandeur- grand and huge palaces etc. described in Hindu scriptures such as Mahabharat and Ramayana were a myth because (the sceptics say) if that was the reality, then why no evidence of those grandiose structures are discovered during excavations of ancient sites. They cite the examples of ancient Greek and Roman structures such as Parthenon, Athens (5th century BCE) and the Colosseum, Rome (70-80 CE) still standing. Due to ignorance of facts of history, many Hindus are hard put to respond meaningfully and are forced to be on the defensive. To set the record straight let's see what Dr A.L.Basham, historian and Indologist has to say in this regard in his celebrated master piece *Wonder That was India*. He writes, 'The utilitarian brick buildings of the Harappa Culture, strong and competent though they were, had apparently little aesthetic merit......... With the exception of the walls of Rajagrha, which also have no artistic value, we have no significant architectural remains between the Harappa period and that of Mauryas. This is due to the fact that few buildings were made of stone during this time.

Megasthenes mentions that the palace of Chandragupta Maurya, though very large and luxurious, was built of carved and gilded wood, and the earliest stone buildings to have survived were evidently modelled on wooden originals. We must not assume from the almost complete lack of significant material remains that the Indian buildings in the Mauryan period, or even before, were mean [sic] or primitive. The Mauryan monolithic columns prove that the craftsmen of those days had a thorough mastery of working in stone, and if the great cities of Mauryan times were mainly built of wood we must attribute this chiefly to the comparative scarceness of stone in the Gangetic plain and to the abundance of timber.....'[1] That puts the matter in proper perspective. Huge and grandiose palaces and other structures described in scriptures were constructed of wood due to its abundance in Gangetic plain, in the form of dense forests. Wood being biodegradable, wooden structures, howsoever strong and sturdy would leave no evidence after a few centuries not to speak of millennia. The great Stupa at Sanchi is believed to be the oldest stone structure in Bharatvarsh. It was constructed by the Mauryan emperor Ashok in 3rd century BCE.

So as to leave no doubt in this regard whatsoever, here is what Dr D.N.Shukla says in his 'Vastu - Sastra Hindu Science of Architecture' - 'Visvakarma-Vastusastra:- .... The whole work consists of eighty-seven chapters in about 1800 verses i.e. more than 3500 lines. The following tabulation of the chapters and their subjects will give a bird's eye view of the subject treated in this manual:

Chapter 4. It deals either the men and material to be employed in Vastu. The chief material being wood, it is going to the forests and bringing the timber for buildings from them [sic] .... '[2]

Having settled the matter of 'lack of evidence' of grandeur of ancient structures in Bharatvarsh, let's return to the illustrative example of the great heights scaled by Hindus in art and architecture, viz caves at Ajanta and Ellora. To emphasize the importance of these caves, it can be stated without fear of contradiction that if a Hindu has the option to visit one and only one place to feel proud of his ancient heritage, he must choose Ajanta and Ellora.

Ajanta Caves

Ajanta Caves are a group of 30 rock cut caves situated in the Aurangabad district of Maharashtra state. Oldest of the caves were created in the 2nd century BCE (Satavahan dynasty) and the latest ones in the 5th century CE (Gupta period and Vatakata dynasty). These caves are UNESCO world heritage site. UNESCO citation states: 'Ajanta Caves exemplifies one of the greatest achievements in ancient Buddhist rock-cut architecture. The artistic traditions at Ajanta present an important and rare specimen of art, architecture, painting, and socio-cultural, religious and political history of contemporary society in India. The development of Buddhism manifested through the architecture, sculptures, and paintings is unique and bears testimony to the importance of Ajanta as a major hub of such activities. Further, the epigraphic records found at Ajanta provide good information on the contemporary civilization.'[3]

These caves have the character of Buddhist monasteries (*viharas*) and worship halls (*chaityas*). Caves have been decorated with intricate carvings and their walls and ceilings have been decorated with beautiful elaborate paintings depicting the past lives of Buddha (*Jatak* tales) and scenes from everyday lives of common people. Several caves have idols of Buddha. A glimpse of the carvings, paintings and idols are presented in the plates.

Ellora Caves

It is a complex of 34 rock cut caves comprising Hindu (17), Buddhist (12) and Jain (5) monasteries and temples, situated in the Aurangabad district of Maharashtra state. These caves date from 600 to 1000 CE (Rashtrakuta Dynasty). It is a unique example of the Sarva Dharm Sambhav (equal respect for all religions) motto of Sanatan.

It is also a UNESCO World Heritage site. UNESCO citation states: 'These 34 monasteries and temples, extending over more than 2 km, were dug side by side in the wall of a high basalt cliff, not far from Aurangabad, in Maharashtra. Ellora, with its uninterrupted sequence of monuments dating from A.D. 600 to 1000, brings the civilization of ancient India to life. Not only is the Ellora complex a unique artistic creation and a technological exploit but, with its sanctuaries devoted to Buddhism, Hinduism and Jainism, it illustrates the spirit of tolerance that was characteristic of ancient India.'[4]

Hindu caves in general house images of Hindu Gods and Goddesses carved on the cave walls.

Buddhist caves are monasteries (*vihara*) with prayer halls, multi storey buildings with living quarters, sleeping quarters, kitchens etc. Some caves have carvings of Gautam Budh.[5]

Five Jain caves belong to the Digamber sect and have images of lord Mahavir and lord Bahubali.[5]

Kailashnath Temple

Of all the Ellora caves, the most remarkable is cave no.16 - Kailashnath temple dedicated to lord Shiva. It is a huge temple complex comprising the central courtyard housing the temple, mandaps, halls, arcades, pillars, rooms, windows etc.

Unique feature of the temple complex is that it has been carved out by chiselling away a huge single rock top to bottom rather than the usual bottom to top approach. As the sculptors (must be in hundreds at any given time) would have gradually proceeded downwards, they would have carved out the halls, rooms, corridors, arcades, columns, victory towers, animals (elephant, lion), images of gods and goddesses carved on walls, panels with intricate carvings depicting stories from Ramayana and Mahabharat and the temple itself. The block of rock carved out for temple would have been further hollowed by chiselling out the rock from within creating columns, sanctum sanctorum (*garbh grah*) and the *Shivalingam*.

It is estimated that 1.5 to 2 million cubic feet of rock would have been dug out. Mystery persists as to how and where such a mammoth quantity of dug up rock debris would have been disposed of as there is no evidence of such pile up of rock debris nearby.[6]

We can imagine the enormous challenges that the chief architect(s)/engineer(s) would have faced in converting the concept into reality, leading a team of hundreds and possibly thousands, ensuring coordination and quality control at each step.

What tools the sculptors would have used? Is it conceivable that this whole project could have been accomplished using just the chisels and hammers? Answer to this puzzle (and the one about disposal of huge volume of rock debris) may never be known.

Ajanta Caves

Ajanta Cave 1 (Photo Source: Wikipedia – Public domain)

Ajanta Cave 1 (Photo Source: Wikipedia – Public domain)

Ajanta Cave 4 (Buddha)

Ajanta Cave 10 – Chaitya (Photo Source: Wikipedia)
https://commons.wikimedia.org/wiki/File:Ajanta_caves_aurangabad_14.JPG#mw-jump-to-license

Ajanta Cave 11 – Buddha (Photo Source: Wikipedia)
https://commons.wikimedia.org/wiki/File:Buddha_at_Ajanta_Caves.JPG#mw-jump-to-license

Panoramic view of Ellora caves (Photo Source: Wikipedia) https://commons.wikimedia.org/wiki/File:Ellora_caves,_view_from_Cave_29_(Hindu).jpg#mw-jump-to-license

Ellora – Kailasa Temple panoramic view (Photo Source: Wikipedia) https://en.wikipedia.org/wiki/File:Kailash_temple_(Ellora_cave_no_15)_at_Verul.png#mw-jump-to-license

Ellora – Kailasa Temple – Victory Tower (Photo Source: Wikipedia)
https://commons.wikimedia.org/wiki/File:Kailasa_Temple,_Ellora,_Aurangabad,_Maharashtra,_India_(2018).jpg#mw-jump-to-license

Ellora – Kailasa Temple (Photo Source: Wikipedia)
https://commons.wikimedia.org/wiki/File:Ellora_cave16_001.jpg#mw-jump-to-license

Ellora – Kailasa Temple (Photo Source: Wikipedia)
https://en.wikipedia.org/wiki/Ellora_Caves#/media/File%3AIndra_Sabha_Ellora_Temple_Maharashtra_India.jpg

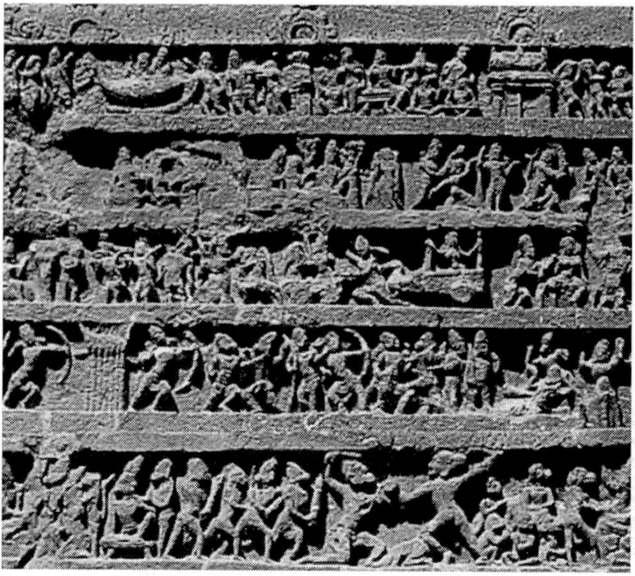

Ellora–Kailasa Temple–Ramayana Panel (Photo Source: Wikipedia) https://en.wikipedia.org/wiki/Ellora_Caves#/media/File%3AEllora_Cave_16_si0300.jpg

Mahabharata Panel (Photo Source: Wikipedia Commons)

Dance (*Nritya Kala*) and Performing Arts (*Abhinaya Kala*)

2500 years back Bharat Muni composed a treatise on dance and performing arts called *Natya Shastra* (Art of theatre, dance and drama). In its 36 chapters and 6000 *shlokas* it describes and enunciates, in details, about performing arts of music, dance and acting. It is perhaps the only treatise of its kind ever written.

We will now discuss, in some detail, three aspects of Hindu civilization viz. Ethics and moral principles, science & mathematics and economic, administrative and justice systems.

Ethics and Moral Principles of Hindu Society

Every society has some fundamental principles as the bedrock on which the structure of the society stands and grows over time. These principles determine the nature of the society; societies based upon high moral and ethical principles grow into great civilizations.

In most of the other ancient kingdoms, the king was considered as a representative of God, divinely mandated to rule over his subjects. The king could do no wrong was the motto. As such, there was no question of any code of conduct for him. Bharatvarsh was perhaps the only exception, where even kings had a code of conduct to follow.

In other lands, wars between kingdoms were fought without any rules; vanquishing the enemy by any means was the sole objective. Not so in Bharatvarsh. For fighting the enemy on the battlefield, strict rules were laid down. Let's discuss these two aspects of ancient Hindu moral and ethical code viz. duties of a king (*raj dharma*) and code of war *(yudh niti)* in some details.

Duties of a King

At the end of Mahabharat war, Shri Krishna directed Yudhishthir to go to Bhishma Pitamah, lying on the bed of arrows, and seek his wisdom regarding the duties and conduct of a king. Bhishma's sermon about the code of conduct for kings (*raj dharma*) is included in the *Shanti Parva* of *Mahabharat*. Some excerpts:[7]

1. Righteous path is the only correct path for a king; a righteous king enjoys good fortune in this life as well as the afterlife.

2. A king who is virtuous, is in control of his thoughts and actions, is soft hearted, pious, of pleasing disposition and of generous nature will have his kingdom endowed with good fortune.

3. A king who is too soft in his dealings is often not taken seriously by his officers and they even tend to ignore his orders. On the other hand, a king with too strict and harsh approach tends to make his officers anxious and on the edge. Hence, a wise king should be flexible in his approach i.e. should be soft or strict as the situation demands.

4. A king indulgent in vices falls in esteem in the eyes of his subjects (hence a wise king keeps away from vices).

5. A wise king adopts policies which are in the best interest of his subjects (even if those are against his own inclination).

6. The king should adopt a formal demeanour in his dealings with his officials because too much informality may lead them to cross their limits, they may disrespect the king and may indulge in insubordination. They may become negligent in discharging the assigned duties. They may reveal the weaknesses of the king. They may even seek unreasonable favours from him (which the king may not be inclined to grant but may find difficult to refuse because of their being too close to him). They may indulge in corrupt practices and subvert the interests of the kingdom. In king's court they pretend to be friends of the king and laugh off any reprimand by him.

7. Kingdom comprises of seven constituents viz. the king, ministers, friends (allies), treasury, the state (physical boundaries), castles and the army. Anyone working against any of these constituents, be it a teacher (guru) or a friend deserves death penalty.

8. Welfare of his subjects is the supreme duty of the king. Defence of righteousness and straightforward demeanour are appropriate for the king.

9. Statecraft has six aspects viz. treaty (*sandhi*) with a more powerful adversary, offence (*vigrah*) against an equal adversary, attack against a weaker adversary, defensive retreat and lying low in hiding (*aasan*) when under attack from a more powerful adversary, deceptive posturing i.e. outwardly friendly but planning offensive action on the sly (*dvaidhibhava*), seeking help from another friendly king when attacked (*samashray*).
10. The king should strive to maximize the wealth of the kingdom (because nothing good can be done for his subjects without financial resources). He should strive to dispense justice like the God of death (*Yamraj*) and create wealth like the God of wealth (*Kuber*).
11. Those of the society who can't fend for themselves (indigent or otherwise helpless) should be looked after by the king.
12. The king should deprive the crooks of their wealth by imposing heavy financial penalties (to restrict their crooked activities) and should reward the righteous financially.
13. The king should appoint as his ministers, persons with the following qualities: he should be gallant and pious, loyal and steadfast, never betraying or defecting to the enemy. He must be healthy and wellmannered, one who, while guarding his

own honour, also upholds the honour of others. He should be committed to his duties, wellread, learned, and worldlywise; capable of identifying and keeping under watch the enemies of the state; and resolute, unwavering in his commitment to the king and the kingdom. To the ministers thus appointed, the king should provide the same level of comfortable and opulent lifestyle as he led himself. He should share everything with his ministers (i.e. lifestyle etc.) except for two things - sovereignty and the power to issue orders and decrees.

14. Just as a child dwells fearlessly in his father's house, so should the people move around fearlessly in his kingdom.

15. King should not treat his enemies, even though weak, with disdain because small fire can spread fast, and a little poison can be lethal.

Such were the duties and tasks laid down for kings in ancient Bharatvarsha. It would appear that, at least in theory, the duties and responsibilities attached to the kingship outweighed its pomp and splendour.

Ethics of War

In ancient Bharatvarsh there was a well-established code of conduct for wars between kingdoms. Wars were fought between Kshatriyas who were mandated to strictly adhere to the code (*kshatriya dharma*); any violation invited punishment and social disgrace.

Ethical War (*Dharm Yudh*)

War conducted in accordance with the code was termed as 'ethical war' (*dharm yudh*). According to the code, 'When a conqueror felt that he was in a position to invade the foreigner's country, he sent an ambassador with a message: 'Fight or submit.' 5000 years ago India recognized that the person of the ambassador was inviolable. This was a great service that ancient Hinduism rendered to the cause of international law.'[8]

'Notwithstanding the love of glory and the spirit of heroism which actuated the warrior, recourse was had to war only if the instruments of diplomacy failed to effect the desired end. Genuine attempts were made to avoid armed contests and to keep peaceful relations ....If diplomacy failed to bring about compromise, and if war was provoked, surely there was retaliation. Vigorous preparations were made to vanquish the enemy by attacking the vulnerable points in his line. It was considered no sin to strike the enemy at his weak points.'[9]

Some salient points of the ethical war code:[10]

1. A warrior in armour was not to fight with another who was not in armour.
2. One could fight only one enemy and cease fighting when the opponent became disabled.
3. A charioteer could fight with another charioteer. Similarly, a horse warrior could fight with another

horse warrior. The general rule was that a warrior could fight only with his equal.

4. An opponent whose weapon was broken or who had lost his chariot could not be hit.
5. A warrior who had thrown off his weapon and requested to be spared with folded hands must not be killed. However, he could be taken as a prisoner.
6. Panic stricken and scattered (running away from the battlefield) enemy should not be pursued.
7. It was prohibited to fight those who did not offer to fight or who had hidden themselves in fear.
8. It was prohibited to harm those who came as spectators.
9. Flower and fruit gardens, temples and other places of public worship were not harmed. *

* 'We have the testimony of a foreign ambassador to this country in the fourth century BC. Megasthenes says: 'Whereas among other nations it is usual in the contests of war to ravage the soil and then reduce it to an uncultivable waste, among the Indians, on the contrary, by whom husbandmen are regarded as a class that is sacred and inviolable, the tillers of the soil, even when battle is raging in their neighbourhood, are undisturbed by any sense of danger from the combatants and either side in waging the conflict make carnage of each other but allow those engaged

in husbandry to remain unmolested. Besides they neither ravage an enemy's land with fire nor cut down its trees.'[11]

10. The battle continued till sunset. After sunset, the warriors of both sides could mingle in a friendly atmosphere.
11. A wounded opponent should either be sent to his own home or if taken to the victor's quarters, he should have his wounds attended to by skilled surgeons. After he is healed, he should be set at liberty.
12. After defeating the enemy in battle, and finding them suffering from agony of wounds, the victor should show mercy to them and sympathise with them, by comforting them, taking hold of their hands affectionately.

According to the ethics of war, a defeated king or, if he had fallen in battle, his rightful heir was restored to the throne. The vanquished ruler would then serve as a vassal to the victor. Great care was taken not to interfere with the customs and culture of the defeated kingdom, so as not to offend the sentiments of its citizens and risk rebellion. In general, Hindu kings upheld the principle: ruthlessness on the battlefield, but generosity in victory—always with the aim of safeguarding the welfare of the defeated state's people.

War by Deception (*Koot Yudh*)

Opposed to *dharma yudh* was *koot yudh* (war by deception) in which sole objective was to win by employing all means (ethical or unethical). In this kind of war, in addition to weapons, recourse was taken to deception, hypnosis, illusion etc. to confuse and overpower the enemy. As per Kautilya, 'if the enemy practiced *kutayuddha*, the defender must also resort to it...... opponents should be paid in their own coin.'[12] The king should be prepared for *koot yudh* also (even though he may not be inclined for it) so that in the event of the enemy indulging in it, he is not caught off guard and can respond accordingly. Even in *koot yudh*, use of devices such as poison and fire were prohibited, to prevent loss of life and property of civilians, cattle etc.[12]

Though some ancient authorities did permit resort to *koot yudh* under certain circumstances, it was generally held that a king who secures victory by resorting to koot yudh, 'incurs disgrace in this world and sinks into hell.'[13]

Undoubtedly, fighting wars following an ethical code of conduct was the pinnacle of Hindu civilization. However, it is also true that there were kings who had no compunction in resorting to *koot yudh* resulting in ethics succumbing before wickedness.

Before we conclude this section, here is what Dr A.L. Basham has to say in his monumental work - The Wonder That Was India:

'In no other part of the ancient world were the relations of man and man, and man and the state, so fair and humane. In no other early civilization were slaves so few in numbers, and in no other ancient lawbook are their rights so well protected as in the *Arthasastra*. No other ancient lawgiver proclaimed such noble ideals of fair play in battle as did Manu. In all her history of warfare Hindu India has few tales to tell of cities put to the sword or of the massacre of non-combatants. The ghastly sadism of the kings of Assyria, who flayed their captives alive, is completely without parallel in ancient India. There was sporadic cruelty and oppression no doubt, but in comparison with conditions in other early cultures, it was mild. To us the most striking feature of ancient Indian civilization is its humanity.'[14]

Mathematics and Sciences

It is said that for the development of sciences, the human mind should be free to soar in the sky of knowledge. On this basis, Sanatan with its tradition of freedom of thought and constant search for truth and knowledge has been eminently well placed for development of sciences.

From ancient times, Bharatvarsh has produced some of the finest brains in the realm of sciences and mathematics. To name just a few:

i. Charak Rishi (4th century BCE), founder of the science of Ayurveda

ii. Sushruta (1st millennium BCE?), father of the science and art of medicine and surgery

iii. Kanad (6th – 2nd century BCE), who first propounded the atomic theory of matter and coined the term *parmanu* for the smallest unit of matter

iv. Nagarjuna (150-250 CE), who worked in the field of metallurgy, alchemy and medicine

v. Brahmagupta (598-668 CE), astronomer and mathematician

vi. Varahamihir (5th- 6th CE), who made significant contribution to astrology and astronomy

vii. Baudhayan (800 – 500 BCE) who made outstanding contribution to mathematics and geometry

viii. Aryabhat (476 – 550 CE), who is famous for his contributions to astronomy and mathematics

ix. Pothayanar (800 BCE), Tamil poet and mathematician

Of these we will discuss briefly the works of the last three.

Dr A.L. Basham writes - 'The debt of the western word to India in this regard (discovery of decimal system) cannot be overestimated. Most of the great discoveries and inventions of which Europe is so proud would have been impossible without a developed system of mathematics, and this in turn would have been impossible if Europe had been shackled by the unwieldy system of Roman numerals. The unknown man who devised the new system was from the world's point of view, after the Buddha, the most important son of India. His achievement, though easily taken for granted, was the work of an analytical mind of the first order, and he deserves much more honour than he has so far received.'[15]

Maybe we are ignorant of the name of the great mathematician of Bharatvarsh who devised decimal system, but we do know of the names of several others whose monumental achievements in the fields of mathematics and Sciences spread the fame of Hindu civilisation far and wide. Let's have a glimpse into the works of two of such famous sons of Bharatvarsh viz. Baudhayan and Aryabhat and also a lesser known one Pothayanar.

Baudhayan (Sulba-Sutra)

In most civilizations, growth of geometry preceded other branches of mathematics. For example, in Egypt geometry developed due to the need for measurement of land for determination of revenue and estimation of agricultural yield.[16] In India it developed on account of religious needs. In Hindu religious texts, strict guidelines had been prescribed for construction of altars (*vedika*) for sacrificial rituals (*yagna*). Design of the altar depended upon the purpose for which the *yagna* was being performed. Need arose for bricks and tiles of varied shapes and sizes for construction of the altars. Whence grew the science of design and measurement of various shapes viz. *sulba-sutra* (*sulba* literally means cord or rope which was used for measurement; *sulba-sutra* thus means rules for measurement). Physical construction of altars adhering to the strict designs mandated in the scriptures involved precision and construction skills resulting in development of technology for making bricks and tiles of different shapes, architecture and civil engineering. Notwithstanding its origine in the need for construction of religious structures (*vedika*), the mathematics developed in sulba-sutra is for universal application i.e. for construction of non-religious structures as well.[17]

Several *Sulba-Sutras* have survived to this day, the oldest being one created by Baudhayan *rishi* (sage, scholar). Baudhayan is believed to have lived sometime between 800 BCE and 500 BCE[18]. In his SulbaSutra, Baudhāyana describes various geometrical shapes and the methods for constructing them, approaching the subject from the practical perspective of a craftsman or technician, using simple tools such as a cord and a pole. A few examples include[19]:

1. How to construct a square (or rectangle) with specified length of sides.
2. To construct a square whose area is three times the area of a given square.
3. To construct a square equal in area to the combined area of two other squares of different sizes.
4. To construct a square of area equal to the difference between the areas of two given squares.
5. To transform a square into an isosceles trapezium whose shorter side is given as lesser than the side of the square.
6. To construct a triangle (or rhombus) equal in area of a given square.
7. To turn a square into a circle and vice versa.

If any doubts persist about the greatness of Baudhayan and his Sulba-Sutra, those will be dispelled by the following verse:

The proposition that the square on the diagonal of a given square is twice as large as that of the given square.[20]

Today we know the above proposition as Pythagoras theorem. Should it not, more accurately, be known as the Baudhayan theorem?

Aryabhat (Aryabhatiya)

Aryabhat was born in 476 BCE in Kusumpura

(Patiliputra).[21] He was a scholar of mathematics and Science. He created two masterpieces on these disciplines viz. Aryabhatiya and Aryabhat Siddhant. What follows gives a glimpse of the scholarship and profound knowledge presented by Aryabhat in *Aryabhatiya*.

1. Area of a triangle: The product of the perpendicular (dropped from the vertex on the base) and half the base gives the measure of the area of the triangle.[22]

2. Area of a circle: Half of the circumference, multiplied by the semidiameter certainly gives the area of the circle.*[23]

   *[Area of a circle = $1/2 \times 2 \times \pi \times$ radius x radius = $\pi \times (\text{radius})^2$]

3. Volume of a sphere: That area (of the diametral section) multiplied by its own square root gives the exact volume of a sphere.*[24]

   *[Volume of a sphere = $\pi \times r^2 \times (\pi \times r^2]^{1/2} = (\pi)^{3/2} \times r^3 = 5.564 \times r^3$. This gives only appx volume of a sphere. Accurate formula for volume of a sphere was given by Bhaskar II (1150 AD) as follows[25]: Volume of a sphere = 1/6 x surface x diameter = $1/6 \times 4 \times \pi \times r^2 \times 2r = 4/3 \times \pi \times r^3$]

4. Circumference – Diameter ratio: 100 plus 4, multiplied by 8 and added to 62000: this is the nearly approximate measure of the circumference of a circle whose diameter is 20,000.[26] *

*[This gives Circumference/Diameter = 62832/20000 = 3.1416 = π]

5. Reduction of two fractions to a common denominator: Multiply the numerator as also the denominator of each fraction by the denominator of the other fraction; then the given fractions are reduced to a common denominator.[27]*

   * [(a/b) + (c/d) = (ad)/(bd) + (cb/db) = (ad + cb)/bd]

6. Meeting of two moving bodies: Divide the distance between the two bodies moving in the opposite directions by the sum of their speeds, and the distance between two bodies moving in the same direction by the difference of their speeds; the two quotients will give the time elapsed since the two bodies met or to elapse before they will meet.[28]

7. Apparent motions of the stars due to the earth's rotation: Just as a man in a boat moving forward sees the stationary objects (on either side of the river) as moving backwards, just so are the stationary stars seen by people at Lanka (on the equator), as moving exactly towards the west.[29] *

   *This statement of Aryabhat is irrefutable evidence that he believed in the rotation of earth on its axis in contradiction to the general belief that the earth was stationary and the universe was rotating around it.

8. Occurrence of an eclipse: When at the end of a lunar month, the moon, lying near a node (of the moon), enters the sun, or, at the end of a lunar fortnight, enters the earth's shadow, it is more or less the middle of an eclipse, (solar eclipse in the former case and lunar eclipse in the latter case).[30]

As stated earlier, this is just a glimpse into the vast knowledge presented by Aryabhat in the realm of mathematics and astronomy. His works include Mathematics, arithmetic, algebra, plane trigonometry, spherical trigonometry, fractions, quadratic equations, table of sines.

Pothayanar[31]

Pothayanar was a Tamil mathematician and poet who lived around 800 BCE. He is known for devising a practical and simple method to determine the length of the hypotenuse of a right-angle triangle given the lengths of the other two sides. The theorem known after the Greek philosopher Pythagoras (570 - 495 BCE) was still more than 200 years away. Need for the above-mentioned formulation arose in relation to the construction of buildings especially temples. Whereas the Pythagorean method involves squaring of the lengths of the base and perpendicular sides of the triangle, adding them and then determining the square root to arrive at the length of the hypotenuse, the Pothayanar's method involves relatively simple operations viz. division and addition. It states as follows:

Divide the horizontal (base) into eight parts. Discard one part and add the remaining to half of the vertical. The result is the length of the hypotenuse.

We can readily test the correctness of the above formulation vis a vis Pythagorean method:

Base	**Vertical**	**Hypotenuse as per Pythagoras theorem**	**Hypotenuse as per Pothayanar method**
8	6	10	10
18	10	20.6	20.75
110	96	146	144.25
876	545	1031.70	1039
2675	1865	3261	3273
342	546	644	572
1100	1300	1703	1612
1300	1100	1703	1688

As we can see, application of Pothayanar's method gives approximately correct length of the hypotenuse (which is good enough for civil engineering applications) when length of the base is greater than the vertical. However, when the base is lesser, the results are widely off the mark. This problem is solved simply by applying the first part of operation viz. dividing the length into 8 equal parts and discarding one part, to the longer side out of the base and the vertical.

Formulated more than 200 years before Pythagoras, Pothayanar's method is remarkable for its simplicity and practical application, in design and construction of South Indian temple gopurams.

Statecraft, Economy and Judicial System

Hindu civilization reached great heights in the realms of economic policy, statecraft and justice system, as revealed in The Arthashastra (3rd century BCE), a treatise credited to Chanakya or Kautilya (real name Vishnu Gupta). At the outset let it be clarified that the modern meaning of Sanskrit word Arthashastra (arth - wealth, shastra - treatise) is economics. However, in Arthashastra, Kautilya in addition to economics, has expounded on other aspects of statecraft such as - qualities of a good king and his duties, appointment of ministers and departmental heads (qualifications and duties), enforcement of law and order, safeguards for the citizens from oppressors, surveillance and control of public servants, organisation of army, conduct of war (including war by deception - *koot yudh*), methods and means to defeat the enemies of the state (internal as well as external), devices to capture the forts of the enemy, organisation of secret service (appointment of spies, their network and methodology etc.), appointment of ambassadors (*rajdoot*), appointment of revenue officers (*rajasva adhikari*) and their duties, appointment and duties of magistrates (*dandpal*) and much more. In fact, there is no aspect of statecraft which has escaped the attention of Kautilya. It can rightly be considered as a compendium or a guide for kings on how to administer a kingdom smoothly while keeping it safe from internal and external enemies. Excerpts from Arthashastra:

Qualities and Duties of a King (*raj dharma*) [32]

Earlier we had discussed the duties of a king as laid down by Bhishma Pitamah in the Shanti Parva of Mahabharat. Now let's see how Kautilya has expounded on the same topic. The differences between the requirements of the relatively simpler Mahabharat period and more complex times of Kautilya (3rd century BCE) are apparent.

Kautilya Says

A good king should be born of high family. He should be godly (pious), virtuous and truthful. He should respect aged persons and seek their advice to benefit from their experience. He should be decisive and quick in taking decisions, determined and unwavering. He should appoint only capable persons as his advisors/ministers. He should be a stickler for discipline. He should be valorous in the face of his enemies and capable of keeping neighbouring kings in check.

He should have a sharp intellect, strong memory and keen mind. He should be capable of rewarding (the deserving) and punishing (the wrongdoer).

He should have foresight to see dangers ahead and taking timely remedial measures.

He should have the cleverness to decide whether to continue with treaties and agreements or end them. Similarly, whether to continue with war with an enemy or end it (i.e. he should be a good judge of his strengths and weaknesses vis-a-vis his enemy and decide in the best interest of his kingdom).

Kautilya has described, in detail, duties of the king and what should be his ideal daily schedule[33]

The fundamental principle underlying the duties of a good king is described by the following statement - 'In the happiness of his subjects lies his happiness; in their welfare his welfare; whatever pleases him he shall not consider as good, but whatever pleases his subjects he shall consider as good.' That is, the king's well-being lies in the wellbeing of his people (*praja*). The king's actions must be guided by what is good for the people rather than his own whims and fancies.

In his court, his subjects (*praja*) shall have free access to him with their grievances and he shall hear them out without delay. A king who is inaccessible to his people and let's his officials deal with their grievances runs the risk of causing disaffection among the people, thereby becoming vulnerable to his enemies (a kingdom in which the people are dissatisfied and disgruntled is weak).

He must attend to all urgent matters/problems at once because if postponed they become intractable and hard to solve.

Constitution of the Council (of Ministers) and Rules for its Deliberations[34]

All administrative decisions should be deliberated in a 'well formed' council (i.e. comprising competent advisors) before implementation. The deliberations of the council shall be strictly confidential, so much so, the punishment for disclosure of council's deliberations is specified as death. Kautilya says the secrecy is to be maintained till the time for starting the work (decided in the council deliberations) has arrived. He cautions that habits such as carelessness, intoxication and love are major causes for betrayal on part of ministers/advisors. From the above it is obvious that apart from other qualifications for appointment as a minister/advisor, the most important are trustworthiness, fastidiousness, freedom from intoxication and last but not the least, strength of character so as not to succumb in weak moments in relation with women (i.e. not reveal secrets in moments of weakness).

The king should avoid endless deliberations with too many advisors. On crucial matters he should not depend on the advice of a single minister, as such an advice could be wilful and malicious (driven by selfish motives). Advice of two ministers can also be suspect as the two could enter an unholy alliance and overwhelm the king or alternatively there could be a stalemate due to mutual dissension. Hence, says Kautilya, the king should consult three or four ministers as in doing so he will arrive at a satisfactory decision and secrecy is also likely to be maintained (with more than that number of advisors, the deliberations tend to become tedious and endless and prone to breach of secrecy). Having given the above stated general guidelines, Kautilya states: Considering the place, time and circumstances, if need be, the king may consult one or two ministers or may even decide himself.

While considering works to be carried out, the council shall deliberate upon the following aspects viz. Place (where the work is to be carried out), manpower required, finances required, time frame for completion and possible obstacles/dangers during execution of the proposed work. The king could ask for opinion from his ministers individually or collectively. In the process, the king has an opportunity to judge the competence of each of his ministers by the reasoning he gives for his opinion.

As to the strength of his council of ministers, Kautilya says it shall consist of as many as required considering the needs of the kingdom (as per the judgement of the king).

The ministers shall be fully aware of the circumstances of the king as well as his enemies (so that they can work to safeguard king's interests and damage those of his enemies). They shall endeavour to start new projects, bring to completion the ongoing ones and to improve those already completed. They shall enforce strict compliance to orders.

King's ministers are like his eyes (Indra, though possessed only two eyes is called thousand-eyed because of one thousand sages in his assembly).

In emergency situations, he shall call his close advisors as well as full council of ministers and seek their advice. He shall follow the course of action suggested by the majority. *

* This advice of Kautilya is significant because in an emergency there is no scope for detailed deliberations as time is of essence. Hence, the king should apprise full council of the situation and go by the majority decision.

Collection of Revenue[35]

Major sources of revenue for the state as specified in the Arthashastra are: taxes on forts *(durg)*, common citizens (*rashtra*), mines (*khani*), buildings and gardens (*setu*), forests (*vana*), herds of cattle (*vraja*) and roads & traffic (*vanikpath*).

The Arthashastra uses following terms to describe different types of receipts and expenditures:

Receipts may be 1) current, 2) last balance and 3) accidental

What is received day after day is termed current (*vartaman*).

Whatever has been brought forward from year before last, whatever is in the hand of others is termed last balance (*puryushita*).

Whatever has been lost and forgotten (by others), fines levied, compensation realised (for any damage), presents to the king, properties of those fallen victim to epidemics (accrued to the state in absence of any heir) and windfall gains constitute accidental receipts.

Expenditure is of two types - daily expenditure (routine expenditure on day to day running of the administration) and profitable expenditure (investments to generate profits).

What remains after deducting all expenditure already incurred and excluding all revenue to be realised is net balance (*nivi*).

A wise Collector General shall strive to maximize the revenue collection, increase the income and decrease the expenditure.

Accounts Keeping[36]

Superintendent of Accounts shall be responsible for keeping of accounts and account books (*bahikhata*). The account books shall have entries for profit, loss, expenditure, interest/premia (*vyaji*), wages paid, values of gems and commodities, value of gifts received by the king's courtiers, remission of taxes allowed to them, their salaries, gains to wives and sons in the form of gems, land etc., amount of tribute paid to (enemy king) or received from (tributaries) etc.

To supervise the works (account keeping) of various levels, superintendents with corresponding qualifications shall be employed. Rewards and punishments have been specified for the superintendents. Severe punishments have been prescribed for loss suffered by exchequer due to negligence or other demeanour on part of the superintendents. On the other hand, those who have been beneficial for the state are to be rewarded.

Conduct of Public Servants, Rewards and Punishments[37]

Kautilya has laid down, in details, the duties of public servants, rewards for good work and penalties for negligent and the corrupt.

On the subject of corruption by public servants, Kautilya makes an observation as sharp and relevant today as it was in the 3rd century BCE. He states: 'Just as it is impossible not to taste the honey or the poison that finds itself at the tip of the tongue, so it is impossible for a government servant not to eat up, at least, a bit of the king's revenue. Just as fish moving under water cannot possibly be found out either as drinking or not drinking water, so government servants cannot be found out (while) taking money (for themselves).'

Kautilya recommends deployment of spies to identify corrupt amongst government servants. He says, 'Those who attend upon military officers and are noted for their honesty and good conduct shall be spies to watch the conduct of accountants and other clerks.'

Kautilya says that the government servants must work without dissension (conflict) and without concert (collusion) among themselves; each must carry out his work strictly as ordered.

Because, in concert, they tend to collude and conspire to eat up the revenue and when in dissension, they spoil the work.

The government servants shall do nothing without the knowledge of the king. There is only one exception to this rule viz. if any imminent danger to the king is detected, remedial measures shall be taken forthwith without waiting for permission from the king.

The superintendents who meet or exceed the target of revenue collection are to be rewarded and promoted.

Interestingly there is punishment for excessive collection of revenue. Kautilya says: 'Whoever doubles the revenue eats into vitality of the country.' Such an officer is to be warned or even punished depending upon the seriousness of the offence (presumably how much excess taxes he has collected).*

* Such passages in Arthashastra reveal how much importance Kautilya attached to reasonableness of taxation. He believed that excessive taxation was

counterproductive as he says above, it saps the vitality of the country. Elsewhere he has expressed similar sentiments thus: The king should realise taxes from the people in the same way as the bee extracts nectar from the flower i.e. without causing any harm to it.

Concerning Law (justice system, different types of crimes and punishments etc.)[38]

Kautilya has laid down an elaborate legal system - qualifications and appointment of Magistrates (*dandpal*), how the court proceedings are to be conducted, punishments for magistrates who deviate from the guidelines, different types of offences, punishments for the same etc. A few excerpts:

'Three members acquainted with sacred law and three ministers of the king (*amatya*) shall carry on the administration of justice.'

'In virtue of his power to uphold the observance of the respective duties of the four castes and of four divisions of religious life, and in virtue of his power to guard against the violation of dharmas, the king is the fountain of justice (*dharmapravartaka*).'

'Sacred law (Dharma), evidence (*vyavahara*), history (*charitra*) and edicts of king (*rajasasana*) are the four legs of law. Of these four in order, the latter is superior to the one previously named.'

'It is power and power (*danda*) alone which, only when exercised by the king with impartiality and in proportion to guilt either over his son or his enemy, maintains both this world and the next.'

While Kautilya has specified penalties for various types of offences for the citizens, at the same time he has prescribed punishments for misdemeanours on part of state officials and judges. A few samples[39]:

'When a master of a household, a superintendent or an independent officer issues or makes use of unauthorized orders or seals, he shall be punished with the first, middlemost, or highest amercement, or he may be condemned to death, or punished in any other way in proportion to the gravity of his crime.'

'When a judge threatens, browbeat, sends out or unjustly silences any one of the disputants in his court, he shall first of all be punished with the first amercement. If he defamed or abuses any one of them, the punishment shall be doubled. If he does not ask what ought to be asked, or asks what ought not to be asked, or leaves out what he himself has asked.......... he shall be punished with the middle-most amercement.'

'When a judge does not inquire into necessary circumstances, enquires into unnecessary circumstances, makes unnecessary delay in discharging his duty, postpones work with spite, causes parties to leave the court by tiring them with delay, evades or causes to evade statements that lead to the settlement of a case, helps witnesses giving them clues, or resumes cases already settled or disposed of, he shall be punished with the highest amercement. If he repeats the offence, he shall both be punished with double the above fine and dismissed.'

'When a judge or commissioner imposes an unjust fine in gold, he shall be fined either double the amount of the fine, or eight times that amount of imposition which is either more or less than the prescribed limit.'

'When the superintendent of jails puts any person in lock-up without declaring the grounds of provocation, he shall be fined 24 panas, when he subjects any person to unjust torture, 48 panas, ... when he troubles or receives bribes from a prisoner he shall be punished with the middlemost amercement; when he beats a prisoner to death, he shall be fined 1000 panas. ....'

Concerning Marriage, Duty in Marriage, Property of a Woman and Compensation for Remarriage[40]

Kautilya has described different types of marriage thus: Giving away, in marriage, of a maiden (by the parents) (i) for a couple of cows is called *Arsha*, ii) to an officiating priest in a sacrifice is called *Daiva* and iii) after receiving plenty of wealth is termed *Asura*. It is obvious that these types of marriages were arranged by the parents. Further, it is evident that the bride's parents received dowry rather than they giving it. Kautilya's terming third type of marriage viz. after payment of plenty of wealth as *Asura* makes it clear that he disapproved of it.

Apart from the above-mentioned types of marriages, three more types have been specified - iv) *Gandharva* - voluntary union of a maiden with her lover, v) *Rakshasa* - marriage after abduction of a maiden and vi) *Paisacha* - marriage after abducting a sleeping and intoxicated maiden.

Property of Women (*Stridhan*)

'Means of subsistence (*vritti*) or jewellery (*abadhya*) what is called property of a woman. Means of subsistence valued at above two thousand shall be endowed (on her name). There is no limit on jewellery.' A woman was free to use her *stridhan* to support herself and her family if abandoned by her husband. However, normally she could not use her *stridhan* without the consent of her son(s) as they were the heirs to it.

Remarriage

On the death of her husband, the wife could decide to lead a 'pious life' or remarry. In the former case she would receive her *stridhan* at once (if not already in her possession). In case of the second marriage, she would receive it at the time of her re-marriage. However, there is a rider here viz she would receive that part of the *stridhan* which was given to her by her father-in-law, provided she re-marries the man approved by him; otherwise, she would forfeit it.

Interestingly, a woman could re-marry in case of prolonged absence of her husband i.e. abandonment.

Kautilya has laid down clear rules for inheritance of the *stridhan* upon her death - first right of inheritance was of sons and daughters (equal share). In case there were no sons and/or daughters, the husband and other relatives would get what each one had given to her as gift/dowry.

Remarriage of Males

Males were not free to re-marry as they wished, while the first wife was alive. Kautilya has laid down strict rules for it, obviously to safeguard the interests of the first wife. Waiting period specified for different circumstances, before he could re-marry, are:

If the wife is barren or has no male issue - 8 years,

If she bears only dead child - 10 years,

If she gives birth to only female children - 12 years.

Heavy penalties have been specified for violation of above rules.

Sexual Exploitation of Immature (Minor) Girls[41]

Kautilya has prescribed harsh punishments for sexual exploitation of women in general and minor girls in particular. Says he:

'He who defiles a maiden of equal caste before she has reached her maturity shall have his hands cut off or pay a fine of 400 panas; if the maiden dies in consequence, the offender shall be put to death.'

'He who defiles a maiden who has attained maturity shall have his middle finger cut off or pay a fine of 200 panas, besides giving an adequate compensation to her father.'

Three centuries BCE, Chanakya declared - 'No man shall have sexual intercourse with any woman against her will.'

Attitude of a Victorious King[42]

Kautilya has discussed in details various aspects of expansion of his kingdom by a king and his dealings with other kingdoms, inimical or friendly. He has advocated use of all the kinds of means to achieve his objectives viz. *sama* (through pretentious dialogue like an equal with an enemy, persuasion, flattery etc.), *daam* (playing on the greed, bribing, gifts etc.), *danda* (threatening, bullying), *bhed* (spying through spies to know the weaknesses of the enemy, creating confusion and chaos in the enemy territory etc.). Yet, cautions Kautilya, 'He should never covet the land, things, and sons and wives of the king slain by him; he should reinstate in their own estates the relatives of the kings slain. He should install in the kingdom the heir-apparent of the king who has died ...... '

'Whosoever covets the land, things, sons and wives of the kings whom he has either slain or bound in chain will cause provocation to the the Circle of States and make it rise against himself.......'*

*Hence, conquered kings preserved in their own lands in accordance with the policy of conciliation will be loyal to the conqueror.

Greatness of Sanatan/Hindu Civilization

The picture of ancient Bharatvarsh that emerges from the above description is that of a land where high standards of ethics and sense of duty were prescribed even for the kings, progressive in various fields of arts and sciences, a highly developed financial, administrative and legal system in place, protection of women's rights (property, marriage, widow re-marriage, protection against sexual exploitation etc). As already noted, all this was rooted in the freedom of thought and constant search for truth encouraged by the *Sanatan*. Sceptics may argue that all may not have been that great over the time span of thousands of years. Mark of a great civilization is not that it should be uniformly great throughout its entire existence. Even great civilizations may falter from time to time, in the journey over millennia. Important thing is this–when there is fall from the high moral values and principles, does the society adapt to the baser values permanently or yearns and strives to regain the lost higher values. For a great civilization, the high ethical values and principles act like a light house for a ship in turbulent sea. Whatever may have been the state of the Hindu society (high or low) during its over 5000 years journey, the higher principles and values as laid down by Hindu scriptures and epics have continued to inspire Hindus over the ages.

Shri Ram's conduct—in his various roles as son, husband, brother, and friend—remains an enduring ideal even today. This is why he is revered as Purushottam, the ideal person. His wholehearted and respectful engagement with individuals from the lower castes of his time continues to be cited as a model of conduct. Similarly, Shri Krishna's discourse to Arjuna on the battlefield of Kurukshetra—the Bhagavad Gita—is regarded as the pinnacle of Hindu thought and philosophy. The point is this: while few Hindus may have lived up to the lofty ideals set by Shri Ram and Shri Krishna, the very fact that these teachings are upheld as ideals worth striving toward is itself a testament to the greatness of Sanatan and Hindu civilization.

Chapter-3

Hindu Religion/Society: Strengths, Aberrations and Misconceptions

Sanatan/Hindu religion is the only surviving ancient religion which has existed in continuity for over 5000 years and is still going strong. What inherent strengths of Hindu religion/Society made it possible? There are several – freedom of thought and expression, intellectual capacity and creativity, freedom of belief and method of worship to name a few. We have touched upon each of these aspects of Hindus in earlier chapters. Here, we will discuss one strength which sustained Hindu religion/Society during its darkest phase viz. 800 years of foreign subjugation, in some detail.

Every society, over time, undergoes some undesirable aberrations which weaken and degrade it; Hindus are no exception. We will discuss one such aberration which beset the Hindu society and continues to some extent even to this day viz. caste system. We will see how it weakened Hindu society and facilitated subjugation of Hindus by invaders, the consequences of which Hindus suffered for centuries and continue to suffer even today.

We will also discuss some misconceptions about Hindu religion and practices.

Foremost Strength of Hindus – Freedom of Belief

Freedom of belief available to every Hindu is the biggest strength of Hindu religion. Every Hindu is free to perceive the form of God to worship, the way of worship (rituals) etc. So much so, a Hindu can declare themselves an agnostic and yet be part of the Hindu society.

In respect of social customs (*reeti-rivaaz*) also there is no uniformity across the Hindus of different regions. Social customs among Hindus vary widely from caste to caste, sect to sect, region to region. These variations among Hindus of different descriptions are also on account of the freedom of choice available to them. The kind of freedoms enjoyed by Hindus is not available to followers of most other faiths, especially Islam. For Muslims, what to believe, what not to believe, whom to pray and how to pray etc. is all laid down for strict compliance.

In fact, the survival of Sanatan and Hindu religion for thousands of years despite centuries of oppression at the hands of invaders can be attributed to the freedoms available to Hindus. A person not bound by any dogma and free to think for himself can readily adapt to a changed circumstance. Who can truly annihilate the civilization and religion of a people who perceive the

Divine in all things, living and nonliving, and whose way of life and worship is flexible enough to adapt to any circumstance? Invaders destroyed temples, yet Hindus simply created temples within their homes and continued their spiritual pursuit, for there was never any compulsion to visit a temple to worship. In fact, there is no rigid connection between a specific mode of worship and being a Hindu. For being a Hindu, pride and belief in the Sanatan principles and ethics is sufficient. Physical symbols of a religion can be destroyed but none can destroy the faith and beliefs of a people.

Another distinctive characteristic of the Hindus has been the continuous change with time. As discussed earlier, fundamental principles of Sanatan are eternal, however, Hindu religion and civilization have continued to evolve with time adapting to changing circumstances. Not that all changes were for the good of the society; some were retrograde which made Hindu society weaker. Nevertheless, it can be asserted that survival of Sanatan and Hindu religion despite repeated onslaughts from marauders and invaders was essentially due to the propensity to adapt and change according to the needs of the time. During Muslim rule, Hindus adapted many of their customs to meet exigencies of the period. Before arrival of Islam, veil (*parda*) was not common among Hindu women. However, during Muslim rule, veil for women became a compulsion.[1] Customs that originated under duress, born out of the instinct for selfpreservation, gradually hardened into norms. Over time, any deviation from them came to be frowned upon by the community, with little remembrance that these practices had emerged in distressing circumstances and were no longer justified in changed times. The urge to change with times inherent in Hindu psyche did assert in due course and self-correction in respect of some of the undesirable practices did take place from within. One such practice which got abolished was *sati* (burning of the widow along with dead husband). Practices of veil and child marriage have got abolished totally from urban areas and to some extent from rural areas. We Hindus should be proud of our inherent ability to adapt to changing circumstances. As stated earlier, it is this very ability which has sustained us during 800 years of subjugation. On the other hand, there are some other religionists for whom mere suggestion of any change (reforms) acts as a red rag.

Biggest Aberration of Hindu Society – Oppression of Lower Castes

As stated earlier, every society is in a state of gradual but constant evolution with time. As a part of this evolution, the Hindu society changed in ways that were progressive in nature and enriched and uplifted it. Great achievements in various fields, some of which were discussed in the previous chapter brought about such positive changes in Hindu society. However, some changes that took place in the Hindu society became a curse for it, in due course, for example the caste system. It has done tremendous damage to the Hindu society. It weakened it in more ways than one and contributed in a big way to the spread of Islam and Christianity in Bharatvarsh and eventual subjugation of Hindus.

If only one factor is to be cited for spread of Islam in Bharatvarsh and whatever it entailed for Hindus, it will be the caste system. A large segment of society comprising the so-called lower castes, which was unjustly denied its rightful place in society by the powerful upper castes, resulted in creation of a huge pool of dissatisfied and disgruntled masses. This segment was a 'sitting duck' for conversion to Islam, for it offered them, above all, equality which was denied to them in their parent religion. Process of conversion continued unabated for centuries. That explains presence of Muslims in such large numbers in Bharatvarsh.

Thousands of years back, when the structure of the society was rather simple, society was classified into segments (*varna*) based upon the nature of work. Set of people who studied scriptures and performed rituals on various occasions such as birth, death, marriage etc. were called Brahmins. Those who joined the army and defended the state against external aggression came to be classified as Kshatriyas. Those engaged in economic activities such as business and trade were known as

Vaishyas. The remaining groups who provided various essential services for the first three classes, such as farmers, potters, cobblers, washermen, and labourers, were classified as Shudras.

It is said that knowledge is power. Brahmins (and only Brahmins) being repositories of the knowledge in the scriptures, in due course, came to acquire the most exalted and powerful position in the Hindu society. Ksatriyas possessed muscle power and the Vaishyas with the power of wealth also occupied high positions in Hindu society. Shudras, bereft of any kind of power suffered what every powerless suffers - exploitation and oppression. Apart from these four *varnas*, there was another class of people who were, in a way, outside the formal structure of society. Any form of interaction with them was prohibited, so much so, even their shadow was considered as polluting. These people were called untouchables (*achoot*). Hereafter, we will use the term 'dalit' for them.

To begin with, *varna* was determined by the nature of occupation of the person. Progeny were not mandated to follow the occupation of their fathers/ forefathers. Through hard work and merit, they could aspire to belong to a higher varna. There are several examples to support this fact.

In *Treta Yug*, the author of epic *Ramayana*, Valmiki was originally a dacoit, that is his place was outside the society, yet because of his profound scholarship as author of epic *Ramayana*, he attained an exalted position of *Rishi* (saint) in Hindu society.

In *Ramayana*, during his fourteen years sojourn in forests, Shri Ram's congenial and respectful interaction with inhabitants of forests, all of whom could be labeled as outcasts (being outside the formal *varna* hierarchy), was an unambiguous message that no one was to be judged based upon one's vocation and/or position in social order. In fact, his army for attacking Ravana's Lanka comprised totally of tribals - an instance of so-called outcasts taking on the role of *Kshatriyas*.

In *Dwapar Yug* also there were several instances of people belonging to the lower strata of society earning respect and high status based upon their merit. One such example is that of Eklavya. He was a tribal, hence did not belong to any of the *varnas*. As such, as per the prevalent norms, he was a dalit. He wanted to learn and master the art of Archery (*dhanurvidya*). He approached Guru Dronacharya, the foremost master and teacher of martial arts at the time. He was the guru and teacher of Kauravas and Pandavas. Dronacharya declined to take Eklavya as a pupil on the plea that he trained only the princes. Eklavya did not lose heart. Whenever Guru Dronacharya would be instructing Kauravas and Pandavas, Eklavya would clandestinely observe and listen to his instructions intently and practice on his own. In due course he became an expert archer. Once Guru Dronacharya had an opportunity to watch the archery prowess of Eklavya and what he saw left him speechless and worried. Worried because he had vowed to train Arjun to be the greatest archer in the world and now that objective appeared to be in jeopardy for Eklavya was no less accomplished than Arjun. Dronacharya asked Eklavya about his Guru. On Eklavya naming him as his Guru, he asked him to pay his *gurudakshina* (teacher's fee the pupil was obligated to pay at the conclusion of training). With the objective of rendering him ineffective as an archer, Dronacharya asked Eklavya for his right-hand thumb as his *gurudakshina*. Eklavya complied without hasitation and cut off his right-hand thumb and offered to him. Nevertheless, Eklavya continued to be an accomplished archer and was an important warrior in Jarasandh's army. The point of the story is that Eklavya did not face discrimination because he was an outcast or Dalit. Dronacharya declined to take him as a pupil because he trained only the princes, the Kauravas and Pandavas, and not due to Eklavya's social status. In due course, his becoming an important warrior in Jarasandh's army further confirms that in those times, a meritorious outcast could acquire status and respect due to a kshatriya.

Satyavati was daughter of the fisherman Chieftain (*Dashraj*), hence outside the four recognized varnas. Yet King Shantanu married her and made her his consort.

Above examples establish beyond doubt that in ancient Bharatvarsha, varna by birth did not prevent anyone from great accomplishments based upon merit and hard work. Nevertheless, the balance of power in the *varna* hierarchy was heavily loaded against the lowest and for centuries they suffered the fate that weak invariably suffer viz oppression and exploitation at the hands of more powerful. Some of the serious consequences of the aberrations of varna system, suffered by Hindu society, need elaboration:

1. A fragmented society is inherently weak. The onus to defend the state against external aggression rested solely on kshatriyas; people belonging to other varnas, especially the shudras, who were the most numerous, were strictly prohibited from carrying arms. Had Hindu society not been so fragmented and everybody, irrespective of the *varna*, was allowed to fight to defend the kingdom, history of Bharatvarsh would have been different.

2. As mentioned earlier, one major contributing factor for spread of Islam and Christianity in Bharatvarsh was the existence of oppressed classes (shudras and dalits). Conversion to Islam offered them an easy option to escape from the oppression they were being subjected to in their parent religion. No wonder, the ancestors of most of the Muslims (and Christians) in Bharatvarsh were hindu shudras or dalits.

3. People belonging to *varnas* other than Brahmins, especially shudras, were strictly prohibited from studying scriptures; doing so invited severe punishment. Consequently, a large segment of society remained backward and unenlightened. Apart from their traditional vocation, shudras were bereft of any other knowledge. For any society to be progressive, it is imperative that most of its members should be exposed to knowledge. This was denied to Hindu society for centuries.

As noted earlier, fragmentation of the Hindu society based on caste and oppression of the lower castes is the single most important factor responsible for many of the catastrophic situations faced by the Hindu society in earlier times (remnants of some of which persist even to the present day). Considering the gravity of the matter, we will dwell upon this further in subsequent chapters.

Existence of Numerous Gods and Goddesses and Practice of Worshipping Animals and Inanimate Objects – A Misconception

As already discussed, every Hindu is free to choose the form of God for worship and mode of worship. Essentially every Hindu worships a formless (*nirakaar*) God. Worshipping a formless God is difficult for a lay person; a symbolic physical representation makes it easier to concentrate and connect with God. That physical symbol could be a tree [example - *peepal* (sacred fig tree)], a plant (*tulsi* - holy basil), a river (*Ganga, Yamuna, Narmada, Cauveri*), an animal (cow, serpent), celestial object (Sun, Moon, Stars) or a statue in human form. To non-Hindus it may seem rather bizarre, but for a Hindu it is most natural because one of the fundamental principles of the *Sanatan* is that God is all pervasive (*sarvavyapi*); He is present everywhere and in everything - living or non-living. It being so, a Hindu can readily perceive presence of God in any and every object around. In addition, Hindus were the first to realise the importance and significance of natural elements such as trees and plants, rivers, earth, air etc. for humanity. Worshipping these natural elements was a form of thanksgiving and a commitment for their preservation and conservation.

How do we explain the existence of numerous Gods/Goddesses *(devi/devata)* in the pantheon of Hindu religion? *Sanatan* and Hindu religion is the only religion in continued existence for over 5000 years. No wonder, with the kind of freedom available to Hindus to visualise the form of God for worship, over time, different forms perceived have become enormous. However, it is important to emphasize that whatever physical form of God a Hindu may worship, basically they have the one and the same omnipotent and omnipresent God in their thoughts.

These deeper aspects of Hindu religion are beyond comprehension of non-Hindus. Non-Hindus (many ignorant Hindus too) mock and make fun of these aspects of Hindu religion. We should ignore them in the same way as a learned person ignores the foolish utterances of an ignorant.

Seemingly Unbelievable and Strange Descriptions in Scriptures (*Puranas*)

Over thousands of years of continuous existence of *Sanatan* and Hindu religion, scholars (*rishi, muni*) have created a vast pool of knowledge in the form of Vedas, Upanishads, Puranas, epics (Ramayana and Mahabharat) and much more. All these are repositories of knowledge about history, science, human nature and behavior etc. To explain deep and complex concepts to layman, the ancient scholars resorted to the use of symbolism and make-believe scenarios, which, if taken literally, may seem rather odd. On the other hand, it is also possible that from time to time, many bizarre and irrational narratives may have been interpolated in the original texts. Every Hindu has the freedom to pick and choose the gems of knowledge and enlightenment from the enormous treasure and ignore what seems irrational and bizarre.

Pathetic State of Cleanliness of Hindu Temples and Places of Pilgrimage

One factor common to a mosque, a church, a gurdwara, a Buddhist monastery or a synagogue is this - they all are in a state of reasonable cleanliness befitting a place of worship. Alas, same can't be said about many of the Hindu Temples and pilgrim places. How can the 'abodes of God' be filthy? Hindus and Hindu organizations must ponder over this issue and take necessary remedial action. In this regard, we can learn from the Sikh community. Every Sikh, rich or poor, ordinary or eminent considers doing physical service (*karseva*) in a gurdwara a duty and an honour. So much so, they do such chores as sweeping the gurdwara premises, cleaning dirty utensils or handling shoes of the visitors willingly and with pleasure. If the same passion can be ignited among Hindus, our temples and pilgrim places can be transformed. Considering the magnitude of the task, it can only be undertaken by Hindu social organizations. At present there are several active Hindu organizations who can undertake this noble task. They should deploy volunteers at temples and pilgrim places such as Bananas ghats, Har-ki-Paudi at Haridwar, who should try to instill a feeling among the visitors, that brooming or sweeping the temple premises or the ghats amounts to service of God. At all such places adequate numbers of cleaning appliances (brooms etc.) should be available. If this campaign is undertaken in right earnest, a futuristic scenario in which every visitor, rich or poor, to a temple or bananas ghat or *har-ki-paudi*, picks up a broom and sweeps some dirty area of the place, as a mark of devotion and service to God, is very much in the realm of possibility. Our temples and pilgrim places will become models of cleanliness of which every Hindu will feel proud of.

Chapter-4

Hindus vs Followers of Other Religions

Since ancient times, Hindus have been peace loving, intellectual, creative and progressive. Therefore, Bharatvarsha scaled great heights in every sphere of human endeavor, excelling in spirituality with the Vedas, Upanishads, Puranas, Ramayana, Mahabharata (Gita) and the Tirukkural of the Tamil Sangam tradition; in science and mathematics through the genius of Sushruta, Charaka, Aryabhata, Baudhāyana, Varāhamihira, Brahmagupta, Nāgārjuna, and Bhaskara II; in economics with the works of Kautilya and Thiruvalluvar; in diplomacy and ethics through the wisdom of Shri Krishna, Vidura, and Kautilya; in literature through the creations of Vyasa, Valmiki, Kalidasa, Ashvaghosha, Bhāsa, Shudraka, Vishakhadatta, Vishnu Sharma, and Thiruvalluvar; in grammar through Pāṇini; in performing arts through Bharata Muni; and in education through the great universities of Nalanda and Takshashila—achievements that together stand as a testament to the unmatched intellectual and cultural brilliance of this civilization.

1st century BCE onwards, Bharatvarsh was a major exporter of spices (especially black pepper), pearls, diamonds, precious stones, ivory, silk, spikenard (a rare Himalayan plant used in preparation of perfumes, beauty products and medicines), malabathrum plant leaves (used for making ointments), saffron etc. Roman women were crazy after Indian pearls, muslin and silk. So much so, 'the frenetic pursuit of luxury in the Roman world aroused the indignation of a section of the ruling class and was a theme of animated debate in the Roman senate. Pliny not only condemned 'the insatiable women's craving for luxuries' but also lamented that this led to a drain of 100 million sesterces of gold from Rome each year, half of it to India alone. Despite an element of exaggeration in Pliny's account, there is little doubt that the Romans sent to India a large quantity of gold and silver coins.' [1]

No wonder, Bharatvarsh was one of the most prosperous lands in the world and its fame and name reached far and wide. Several foreigners came to see for themselves the glory of Bharatvarsh - Fa Hien, Hiuen Tsang, Ibn Battuta, Marco Polo, Megasthenes, Al-Baruni to name a few. Foreign students came from far and wide to study at Nalanda and Takshila universities. Also came others whose aim was not to see the glory of Bharatvarsh or to learn from it; it was to plunder and desecrate this great ancient land.

Arrival of Christianity and Islam

Over time, people professing other religions viz.

Muslims, Christians, Jews, Parsis came. Additionally, different beliefs and ways of worship branched out from Hindu religion (for which there was full freedom, as already discussed), which in due course developed into separate religions viz. Buddhism, Jainism and Sikhism. Bharatvarsh has been home to peoples professing all major religions of the world and Hindus have treated them consistent with Sanatan's fundamental moto - *Sarva Dharm Sambhav* (equal respect for all religions). Yet, there has been an unfortunate, long history of conflict between Hindus and Muslims. To understand why Hindus did not face such conflict with any other religious group say Christians, we must go back in history and examine the process of arrival of these two religions (Islam and Christianity) in Bharatvarsh and the conduct and behavior of these religious groups subsequently.

Let's first consider the arrival of Christianity. It is believed Christianity was first brought to Bharatvarsh by St. Thomas who was one of the twelve apostles of Jesus. He came first to the kingdom of the Indo-Parthian king Gondophernes I who ruled in the 1st century CE in northwest Bharatvarsh (now part of Afghanistan and Pakistan) and propagated Christianity there.[2] In 52 CE he reached Malabar (present day Kerala) most probably by sea route.[3] He first initiated Jews of Malabar into Christianity and then extensively propagated Christianity in that region. Gradual spread of Christianity continued and by 600 CE it had taken roots in Malabar and Tamil regions. Point to be noted is that Christianity came to Bharatvarsh in an unobtrusive and peaceful manner and there was no significant opposition to it from the rulers or common people.

Let us now consider arrival of Islam. Arab traders visited Konkan and Malabar, by sea route, even before birth of Islam. However, after the emergence of Islam, these traders, in addition to the goods to be traded, brought with them the ideology of Islam.

In north of Bharatvarsh, Islam arrived not through traders but through invaders. The first invader was Mohammad bin Qassim, who in 711 CE came up to Sindh. Islamic invasions continued from west, however, Hindu kingdoms managed to prevent their advance beyond Sindh. Then came Mahmud Ghaznavi in 1001 CE. He attacked repeatedly and in 1025-1026 CE he attacked Gujarat where he plundered the immense wealth of Somnath temple and destroyed it. Primary objectives of Ghaznavi's repeated invasions were i) to desecrate and destroy Hindu Temples with a view to hurt and humiliate Hindus and ii) to plunder the immense wealth of Bharatvarsh. Ghaznavi carried out seventeen invasions. 'It is said that from Nagarkot alone he plundered 700000 gold dinars, 700 mans* of gold and silver plates, 200 mans in pure gold ingots, 2000 mans of unwrought silver and 20 mans of various jewels, including pearls, corals, diamonds and rubies.'[4]

* 1 man = 37 kg appx

Invasions and plunder continued unabated. Then came Mohammad of Ghor. Mohammad of Ghor or Mohammad Ghori was a ruler of Ghor region of present-day Afghanistan. He repeatedly attacked Indian kingdoms in a bid to expand his empire eastward. In one such campaign, he fought several battles with Prithviraj Chauhan, who was a Rajput king of Chauhan dynasty with his capital at Ajmer, in present day Rajasthan. As per historians, Chauhan defeated Ghori in the first battle of Tarain in 1191. He captured Ghori but let him go unharmed, undoubtedly following the ethics of war which mandated humane treatment by the victorious king towards the defeated. Ghori returned with a bigger army next year and defeated Chauhan in the second battle of Tarain (1192). He captured Chauhan, first blinded him and then killed him[5], for he was not bound by any ethical code. Defeat of Chauhan is seen as a watershed event in Indian history, which lead to establishment of Islamic rule in India. Had Chauhan realised the risk of sparing Ghori and had executed him, in what ways India's history would have been different is a moot point.

It is pertinent to quote Dr B.R. Ambedkar from his monumental book *Pakistan or The Partition of India*:

'These Muslim invasions were not undertaken merely out of lust for loot or conquest....... there is no doubt that striking a blow at the idolatry and polytheism of Hindus and establishing Islam in India was also one of the aims of this expedition.'[6]

'Muhammad of Ghazni also looked upon his numerous invasions of India as the waging of a holy war.'[7]

'The methods adopted by the Muslim invaders of India are not less significant for the subsequent history of India than the object of their invasion.'[8]

Dr Ambedkar has extensively quoted other authorities viz. Dr Murray Thurston Titus [*Indian Islam - A Religious Study of Islam in India* (1930)] and Stanley Lane-Pool [*Medieval India* (1903)] to illustrate how the invaders driven by bigotry and religious zeal perpetrated untold miseries on Hindus. The reader is urged to refer to Dr Ambedkar's book for a better appreciation of those horrific times (for Hindus). The following excerpts are illustrative of the general condition of Hindus during Muslim rule:

'It was left to Auragzeb to make a final attempt to overthrow idolatry. The author of *Ma' athir i - Alamgiri* dilates upon his efforts to put down Hindu teaching and his destruction of temples in the following terms:

'In April AD 1669, Aurangzeb learned that in the provinces of Thatta, Mullan and Benaras, but especially in the latter, foolish Brahmins were in the habit of expounding frivolous books in their schools, and that learners, Muslims as well as Hindus, went there, from long distances ...... The 'Director of the faith' consequently issued orders to all the governors of provinces to destroy with a willing hand the schools and temples of the infidels, and they were enjoined to put an entire stop to the teaching and practising of idolatrous worship ..... Later it was reported to his religious Majesty that the Government officers had destroyed the temple of Bishnath at Benaras.'

As Dr Titus observes:

'Such invaders as Muhammad and Timur seem to have been more concerned with iconoclasm, the collection of booty, the enslaving of captives, and the sending of infidels to hell with the 'proselytizing sword' than they were with the conversion of them even by force. But when the rulers were permanently established the winning of converts became a matter of supreme urgency. It was a part of the state policy to establish Islam as the religion of the whole land.'[9]

'All this was not the result of mere caprice or moral perversion. On the other hand, what was done was in accordance with the ruling ideas of the leaders of Islam in the broadest aspects. These ideas were well expressed by the Kazi in reply to a question put by Sultan Ala-ud-Din wanting to know the legal position of the Hindus under Muslim law. The Kazi said :-

'They are called prayers of tribute, and when the revenue officer demands silver from them they should without question, and with all humility and respect, tender gold. If the officer throws dirt in their mouths, they must without reluctance open their mouths wide to receive it ...... The due subordination of the Dhimmi is exhibited in his humble payment, and by this throwing of dirt into their mouths. The glorification of Islam is a duty and contempt for religion is vain. God holds them in contempt, for he says, 'Keep them in subjugation'. To keep the Hindus in abasement is especially a religious duty, because they are the most inveterate enemies of the Prophet, and because the Prophet has commanded us to slay them, plunder them, and make them captive, saying 'Convert them to Islam or kill them, and make them slaves, and spoil their wealth and property'. No doctor but the great doctor (Hanifa), to whose school we belong, has assented to the imposition of jizya on Hindus; doctors of other schools allow no other alternative but 'Death or Islam'.' (Quoted by Dr Titus).[10]

The objective of the above description is not to retell detailed history of arrival and establishment of Islamic rule in Bharatvarsh; it is to highlight the aggressive and violent manner of their arrival and their objectives viz. plunder, humiliation of Hindus through desecration of temples and spread of Islam by conversion of Hindus by sword.

Christians have also converted large numbers of Hindus to Christianity, but there has never been any significant conflict between them. The reason could be the following: Jesus Christ's whole life and message was based upon kindness, compassion, forgiveness and service to others. Same sentiment underlies the work of Christian missionaries in Bharatvarsh. To motivate the downtrodden sections of Hindu society to convert to Christianity, they offer them all sorts of incentives such as money, free education and medical facilities etc., which they are deprived of otherwise. The motivation behind their charitable activities is not pure service; it is to convert the vulnerable sections of Hindu society. Yet, there can be no valid justification for opposing any activity which benefits the poor and downtrodden.

On the other hand, Muslims came as aggressors and plunderers. They also resorted to large scale conversions, not through service like Christians but by the force of sword. To humiliate Hindus, they desecrated and demolished symbols of Hindu religion, culture and civilization. In 1190 CE Bakhtiyar Khilji destroyed and burnt Nalanda University. The university library, which had thousands of rare manuscripts, was put on fire. It continued to smoulder for months.

As we have noted earlier, Hindus fundamentally believe that everyone is free to choose the form and method of worship one wishes to follow. That's the reason people subscribing to foreign religions did not face any form of resistance or conflict from Hindus, because to them people following those different practices and beliefs were just exercising the right to choose as available to every Hindu. This tolerance and large heartedness which has been their greatest strength became the cause of the worst nightmare and dark period for Hindus and Sanatan.

It is not that Hindu rulers did not resist the invaders. Invaders were motivated by religious zeal and could go to any extent to win. They did not believe in any rules or ethics; deceit, treachery and cruelty were the rules. Whereas Hindu rulers fought with them as they would any other adversary (say another Hindu ruler), following some rules and ethics. No wonder, the ethics and tolerance of Hindus could not withstand the religious bigotry, intolerance and cruelty of the invaders.

How did Hindus and Hindu Religion Survive Muslim Rule?

One pertinent question that arises is this: How did Hindus, Hindu religion, culture and civilization survive the oppressive Muslim rule for centuries? Why did it not disappear totally like several other Civilizations and empires such as Egyptian, Persian, Byzantine empire (Eastern Roman Empire), Sasanian empire to name a few. Some of the possible reasons are as follows:

1. Inherent Nature of Hinduism

As discussed earlier, Hindu religion is not bound by

the dictates of a single book or a prophet. The kind of freedom available to Hindus in matters of religious practices - nature and form of God to worship, rituals to perform etc. is not available to any other religious group. When invaders destroyed their Temples, Hindus made temples in their homes. Since they saw presence of God in every object around them, they worshipped Him in peepal tree (sacred fig), bar tree (banyan) and the Tulsi plant (holy basil) standing in the courtyard of every Hindu home. They prayed to Sun, Moon and Stars. They continued to celebrate their festivals within the confines of their homes, there being no compulsion to mandatory assemble in a place of worship (Temple) for collective celebration.

Additionally, stories from scriptures especially Ramayana and Mahabharat retold to children, generation after generation inspired and kept Hindus grounded in their basic Sanatan beliefs and traditions over centuries.

2. Resistance and Defiance of Hindus

Bharatvarsh is a huge land mass. In the north it extended upto Sind when the first Muslim invaders came. Initially the Muslim invaders were able to conquer territories in the border areas and then gradually extended and consolidated their hold in most of the north - Punjab, Gangetic plains, Rajasthan, Gujarat, Bengal. Yet several Hindu kingdoms - Vijaynagar (south), Ahoms

(Assam), Marathas, Rajputs vigorously resisted Muslim advances. They fought valiantly and even though they might not have succeeded in preventing the eventual spread of the Muslim rule, stories of their heroism and valour, as also the stories of the sacrifices made by Hindu women folk to safeguard their honour [for example the 'jauhar' (jumping into flames) committed by Rani Padmavati of Chittor along with other women, to escape being dishonoured by Allauddin Khalji] told and retold through folklore kept the Hindus inspired, in high spirits and silently defiant.

Sh Sita ram Goel in his 'Muslim Separatism – Causes and Consequences' says: 'Coming to the period following Islamic invasion, Hindu society ….. took pride in Bapa Raval who had humbled the Arabs; in Maharani Nayakidevi of Gujarat and Prithvi raj Chauhan who had defeated Muhammad Ghuri again and again; in Gora and Badal who had recued Rana Ratan Singh from the camp of Alauddin Khalji and then laid down their lives in defence of Padmini and her Chittor; in Harihara and Bukka who had founded the Vijayanagar Empire which stood like a rock against Islamic imperialism for more than two centuries; in Rana Sangram Singh who had crossed swords with Babur; in Maharana Pratap who had defied the mightiest Mughal in the midst of great adversity; in Durgadas Rathor who had despised the wrath of Aurangzeb in defence of his right to give refuge to a rebellious Mughal prince; in Chattrapati Shivaji who devised a new diplomacy and innovated a new art of warfare which finally worsted the most powerful Muslim empire and rolled back the Islamic invasion; in Chhattrasal Bundela and Maharaja Surajmal who revived Hindu rule in the north; in Banda Bairagi who avenged the wrongs done by Muslim despots to Guru arjun Deva, Guru Tegh Bahadur and Guru Gobind Singh; and in Maharaja Ranjit Singh who liberated the Punjab and the North-West Frontier Province from Islamic stranglehold.'[11]

3. Limitations of Muslim Influence and Reach

Even though, nominally the Muslim rule extended over vast areas of Bharatvarsh, considering the limited and primitive means of communication and travel, it is likely that their actual reach and influence would have been limited to the areas around the capital and other urban areas. The life in far flung rural areas would have remained relatively unaffected. As such Hindus in such remote areas would have continued to lead more or less normal lives.

4. Muslim Rulers Needed Well-Educated Hindus for Administration

As the empire expanded, Muslim rulers needed well educated and competent manpower for administration. With their tradition of education, Hindus became the natural choice for such jobs. Accordingly, Muslim rulers had to turn to Hindus perforce. Obviously, they had to tamper their antipathy for Hindus to get their cooperation. It is said that approximately 19% of nobility in Akbar's court consisted of Hindus; Birbal, Raja Todarmal, Raja Mansingh to name a few prominent ones.

Aurangzeb, the most fanatic Mughal ruler was also constrained to employ Hindus. During Aurangzeb's rule, 'Hindus rose to 31.6% of Mughal nobility.'[12]

5. Jizyah

Ironically, Jizyah (a prohibitively high punitive tax levied on non-muslims) which was supposed to be a curse for Hindus, became a saviour of their lives even if at the cost of their wealth and property. When 'Ulama advised SulTan Iltutmish as well as certain other SulTans, not to levy Jizyah on idol-worshipping Hindus but give them an ultimatum of choosing between the alternatives of Islam and death. In view, however, of the overwhelming majority of Hindus, the Sultans dare not do so and rested satisfied with Jizyah.'[13]

Chapter-5

Hindu Nation (*Rashtra*) vs Bharatvarsh (*Desh*)

We generally use the terms 'Nation' and 'Country' interchangeably, whereas, in fact, these terms denote totally different entities. A nation can be defined as a group of people bound together emotionally on account of common civilization, religion, beliefs, language, race, ethnicity or history, not necessarily living in the same geographical area. In general, one or more of the above-mentioned factors are sufficient for existence of a nation. A nation may or may not have a physical boundary. On the other hand, a country is a political entity which has distinct physical boundaries, generally has specified rules and laws (constitution) for its governance, has institutions such as a government, armed forces, judiciary etc. Other differences between a nation and a country are:

The boundaries of a country can change over time by addition or secession of areas. However, since nation is more conceptual than physical, question of any change in its boundaries is not relevant.

Further, a new country can be established or existing one abolished in a relatively short period of time. For example, USSR as a country was established by forcible integration of 15 independent republics by the erstwhile Russia with itself. In the reverse process those annexed areas again became independent countries in 1991.

A nation, however, evolves over a long period of time since emotional integration can't be forced or hurried up.

In case of Bharatvarsh, with numerous languages, different beliefs and customs, regional and sub-regional aspirations etc., what could be the basis of its nationhood? That common basis on which the nationhood of Bharatvarsh has evolved over millennia is Hindu civilization. In other words, Bharatvarsh is a Hindu nation or Hindu Rashtra. This does not imply that people belonging to other religions have no place in Bharatvarsh or they should enjoy lesser rights than Hindus. Bharatvarsh, the country runs according to a constitution which grants equal rights to all citizens (rather somewhat more to non-Hindus). However, Bharatvarsh, the nation follows the Hindu ethos and beliefs. To understand this subtle difference let's consider the situation of Bharatvarsh before independence. There were more than 500 small and big princely states governed by different political systems, in addition to the British India. Bharatvarsh, as a country then was very much different from what it is today; but Bharatvarsh as a Hindu Rashtra was very much in existence then as much as it is today. Hindus of this land were emotionally integrated by the common thread of Sanatan and Hindu civilization. Hindus of north pilgrimaged to Kanyakumari and Rameshwaram *dham* and from south to Varanasi and Badrinath *dham* as much as they do today.

On 15th August, 1947 and thereafter, through integration of princely states and framing of the constitution etc. what was defined was Bharatvarsh the country. Hindu Rashtra existed before that date (it has existed since millennia), it exists today and will continue to exist into future also.

Framers of our constitution also acknowledged this reality - while the constitution they framed declared Bharatvarsh as a secular country, pages of the original constitution have been decorated with sketches of themes representing our ancient Sanatan civilization such as Ramayana, Mahabharat (Bhagvat Gita), Gautam Budh, Mahavir, Nalanda University, Nataraj. Further, country's national emblem is Ashokan Pillar of Sarnath. The mottos of Government of India (*'Satyameva Jayate'*), Supreme Court (*'Yato Dharmastato Jaya)'* and several other government organisations such as Doordarshan ('Satyam Shivam Sundaram'), Indian Army ('Seva Paramo Dharmah'), Indian Air Force ('Nabh Sparsha Deeptam'), Indian Navy ('Shan No Varunah') are in Sanskrit. Public sector projects are initiated with performance of *bhoomi pujan* (earth worship ritual) accompanied by Sanskrit shlokas. Installation of *Sangol* in Lok Sabha recently should be viewed in the same spirit.

From time to time, many Hindus keep demanding that Bharatvarsh be declared a Hindu Rashtra. Such demands are misplaced and born out of misunderstanding because, as discussed above, nations (*rashtra*) are not created by declarations, they evolve over a long period due to factors already discussed. Hence, Bharatvarsh is a Hindu Rashtra and for it being so, no declaration is needed.

Muslim Ummah & Catholic Church vs Hindu Rashtra

Hindu Rashtra can be compared with the concept of Muslim Ummah and Catholic Church. There are 49 Muslim majority countries worldwide. They speak different languages and belong to different ethnicities. Yet the Muslims worldwide have a sense of bonding as a part of Ummah. Many of these countries have mutual disputes, so much so, some of them have been at war with each other. Yet, whenever any issue related to Islam, such as perceived blasphemy is raised anywhere in the world, all Muslims, worldwide rise as one, often violently.

Similarly, Catholics world over, though belonging to different countries are united under the umbrella of Catholic Church headquartered at Rome, led by the Pope. Catholic Christians of Bharatvarsh also feel emotionally attached to the Catholic Church.

If Muslims from different nations and languages can unite as part of the Ummah, and Christians across the world can come together under the Catholic Church, there is no reason why Hindus, heirs to a civilization thousands of years old, cannot unite as part of a Hindu Rashtra.

Characteristics of Hindu Rashtra

1. Hindu Rashtra has no geographical boundaries. Hindus worldwide, who have a sense of belonging to the Sanatan civilization are part of Hindu Rashtra.

2. Hindu Rashtra's tenets have evolved over thousands of years based upon Sanatan beliefs and traditions.

3. It has not been established by any one individual (prophet) and there are no governing rules and regulations.

4. Numerous sects within the fold of Hindu religion such as Arya Samajis (who do not believe in idol worship), Vaishnav (worship God in Vishnu form), Shaiv (worship God in Shiva form), Ramanandi, Swaminarayan, Lingayats, Vokkaligas, Naga sadhus (ascetics) are all part of the Hindu Rashtra. As there are significant differences in the beliefs and ways of worship of these sects, same couldn't be the thread

which binds Hindus of different denominations. That common denominator which unites all Hindus emotionally is our ancient civilization. Hence, the basis of Hindu Rashtra is thousands of years old Sanatan civilization rather than Hindu religion.

5. Freedom of choice in the matter of personal belief available to every Hindu enables different sects of Hindus to coexist without any conflict or discord. For Hindus, any other religious group is just another sect with which they can coexist naturally, in the same way different sects of Hindus coexist among themselves. Hence, concept of Hindu Rashtra has absolutely no conflict with the secular ethos of Bharatvarsh's constitution.

As discussed above, Hindu mind is naturally programmed on the Sanatan principle of '*Sarva Dharma Sambhav*' ('Equal respect for all religions'). What about the followers of other religions? Muslims believe, as a fundamental principle, that Islam is the only true religion and others are inferior. Christians assert that Jesus Christ is the only true son of God, implying that prophets of other religions were inferior to Christ. Hence, followers of other religions are not expected to subscribe to the concept of Hindu Rashtra. However, there are many so called 'secular' Hindus (pseudo seculars) who also oppose the concept of

Hindu Rashtra. Some of them do so because they do not understand the difference between Bharatvarsh the 'nation' and Bharatvarsh the 'country'. Being liberal, they think the concept of Hindu Rashtra is against the secular ethos of the country. Such Hindus should appreciate that there is absolutely no contradiction between Hindu Rashtra and secularism. In fact, Bharatvarsh is an embodiment of secularism since ancient times. *'Sarva Dharma Sambhav'* is nothing but secularism. It is because of this so many religions such as Jews, Parsis and Christians came to Bharatvarsh and got assimilated. However, Muslims came as invaders and oppressors and Bharatvarsh's *Sarva Dharma Sambhav* got shattered. After 600 years of Muslim subjugation and 200 years of British rule, reassertion of Hindu Rashtra is nothing short of a miracle. If Ummah can unite Muslims for Islam, there is no reason why Hindu Rashtra can't unite Hindus. In fact, such a unity is need of the times as we will discuss in the following chapters.

Chapter-6

Hindu Religion and Hindutva

Vinayak Damodar Savarkar (Veer Savarkar) was perhaps the first to expound the concept of 'Hindutva'. This word is derived from Sanskrit words 'Hindu' and 'tatva' (essence) and can be roughly translated as 'Hinduness'. Veer Savarkar in his seminal book 'Hindutva' has discussed in detail as to who is a Hindu. According to him, for being a Hindu there are three characteristics which must be satisfied. First, Savarkar writes, 'The most important factor that contributes to the cohesion, strength and the sense of unity of a people is that they should possess an internally well-connected and externally well demarcated 'local habitation' and a 'name' that could, by its very mention, rouse the cherished image of their motherland as well as the loved memories of their past. We are happily blessed with both these important requisites for a strong and united nation. Our land is so vast and yet so well-knit, so well demarcated from others and yet so strongly entrenched that no country in the world is more closely marked out by the fingers of nature as a geographical unit beyond cavil or criticism, as also is the name 'Hindusthan' or 'Hindu' that it has come to bear. The first image that it rouses in the mind is unmistakably of our motherland and by an express appeal to its geographical and physical features it vivifies it into a living being. Hindusthan meaning the land of Hindus, the first essential of Hindutva must necessarily be this geographical one. A Hindu is primarily a citizen either in himself or through his forefathers of 'Hindusthan' and claims the land as his motherland.'[1]

The first characteristic of a Hindu, as Savarkar describes, is a deep sense of belonging, emotional attachment to, and pride in the physical landmass called Hindusthan (a term he prefers over Hindustan). This sense of belonging may arise from one's own citizenship or from the recognition that one's ancestors were once citizens of Hindusthan. Beyond its physical features—plains, mountains, deserts, rivers—a true Hindu envisions Hindusthan as a living being, as a mother, the motherland.

Secondly, Savarkar says, 'No word can give full expression to this racial unity of our people as the epithet Hindu does. Some of us were Aryans and some Anaryans; but Ayars and Nayars - we were all Hindus and own a common blood..........We feel that same ancient blood that coursed through the veins of Ram and Krishna, Buddha and Mahavir, Nanak and Chaitanya, Basava and Madhava, of Rohidas and Thiruvalluvar courses throughout....... We feel we are a race bound together by the dearest ties of blood and therefore it must be so.......

A Hindu marrying a Hindu* may lose his caste but not his Hindutva. A Hindu believing in any theoretical or philosophical or social system, orthodox or heterodox, provided it is unquestionably indigenous and founded by a Hindu may lose his sect but not his Hindutva - his Hinduness - because the most important essential which determines it is the inheritance of the Hindu blood.'[2] (*undoubtedly here Savarkar is referring to a Hindu marrying a Hindu of another caste which in his time could invite caste ostracization). Use of the term 'Hindu blood' by Savarkar signifies that he considered the second characteristics of a Hindu as being born a Hindu. A born Hindu retains his 'Hinduness' even if he shifts his belief from one sect to another sect of Hindu origin. Thus, a born Hindu embracing Sikhism or Buddhism or Jainism retains his Hindutva. However, a born Hindu converting to Islam or Christianity loses his Hindutva.

Thirdly, Savarkar says, 'A Hindu then is he who feels attachment to the land that extends from Sindhu to Sindhu as the land of his forefathers - as his fatherland; who inherits the blood of the great race whose first and discernible source could be traced from the Himalayan altitudes of the Vedic Saptsindhus and which assimilating all that was incorporated and ennobling all that was assimilated has grown into and come to be known as the Hindu people; and who as a consequence of the foregoing attributes, has inherited and claims as his own the Hindu Sanskriti, the Hindu civilization, as represented in a common history, common heroes, a common literature, common art, a common law and a common jurisprudence, common fairs and festivals, rites and rituals, ceremonies and sacraments. Not that every Hindu has all these details of the Hindu Sanskriti down to each syllable common with other Hindus; but that, he has more of it common with his Hindu brothers than with, say, an Arab or an Englishman. Not that a non-Hindu does not hold any of these details in common with a Hindu but that, he differs more from a Hindu than he agrees with him. That is why Christian and Mohammedan communities who were but very recently Hindus and in a majority of cases had been at least in their first generation most unwilling denizens of their new fold, claim though they might have a common fatherland, and an almost pure Hindu blood and parentage with us, can not be recognized as Hindus; as since their adoption of the new cult they had ceased to hold Hindu civilization (Sanskriti) as a whole. They belong or feel that they belong, to a cultural unit altogether different from the Hindu one. Their heroes and their hero-worship, their fairs and their festivals, their ideals and their outlook on life, have now ceased to be common with ours. Thus, the presence of this third essential of Hindutva which requires of every Hindu uncommon and loving attachment to his racial Sanskriti enables us most perfectly to determine the nature of Hindutva without any danger of using overlapping or exclusive attributes.'[3]

In a nutshell, as per Savarkar, three criteria for being a Hindu (or Hindutva) are:

i) someone who himself/herself is a citizen or whose ancestors were citizens of Bharatvarsh and considers this ancient land as his/her motherland,

ii) being born as a Hindu,

iii) having a sense of belonging and being proud of the ancient culture and civilization (*Sabhyata, Sanskriti*) of Bharatvarsh.

What about the Hindus who themselves or their ancestors emigrated to foreign lands? In this regard, Savarkar says: 'There are hundreds of thousands of Hindus who have settled in all parts of the world......... will this simple fact of residence in lands other than Hindustan render one a non-Hindu? Certainly not; for the first essential of Hindutva is not that a man must not reside in lands outside India, but that wherever he or his descendants may happen to be he must recognize Sindhusthan as the land of his forefathers. .... If his ancestors came from India as Hindus he can not help recognizing India as his Pitribhumi. So this definition of Hindutva is compatible with any conceivable expansion of our Hindu people. Let our colonists continue unabated their labours of founding a greater India, a Mahabharat to the best of their capacities and contribute all that is best in our civilization to the upbuilding the humanity. Let them enrich the people that inhabit the earth from pole to pole with their virtues and let them in return enrich their own country and race by imbibing all that is healthy and true wherever found. So long as ye, O Hindu look upon Hindusthan as the land of your forefathers and as the land of your prophets and cherish the priceless heritage of their culture and their blood, so long nothing can stand in the way of your desire to expand. The only geographical limits of Hindutva are the limits of our earth.'[4]

Hindutva vs Hindu Religion

We have earlier differentiated between Sanatan and Hindu religion; now let's discuss the difference between Hindu religion and Hindutva. Let's see what Savarkar has to say in this regard. He says: 'There would have been no serious objection raised against the cultural aspect of Hindutva too, but for the unfortunate misunderstanding that owes its origin to the confusing similarity between the two terms Hindutva and Hinduism. .... Hindutva is not identical with Hindu Dharma; nor is Hindu dharma identical with Hinduism.'[5]

He explains the difference between Hindu religion and Hindutva by an example: 'We have tried to make it clear that Hindutva is not to be determined by any theological tests. Yet we must repeat it once more that the Sikhs are free to reject any or all things they dislike as superstitions in Sanatandharm, even the binding authority of the Vedas as a revelation. They thereby may cease to be Sanatanis, but can not cease to be Hindus. Sikhs are Hindus in the sense of our definition of Hindutva and not in any religious sense whatever. Religiously they are Sikhs as Jains are Jains, Lingayats are Lingayats, Vaishnavas are Vaishnavas; but all of us racially and nationally and culturally are a polity and a people, one and indivisible, most fitly and from times immemorial called Hindus.'[6]

Hindu religion's fundamental basis is religious faith and belief whereas Hindutva is a concept which encompasses Bharatvarsh's ancient culture, civilization and history. On this basis the Hindus, Sikhs, Jains, Buddhists, Arya Samajis and numerous other sects of Hindus may have different religious beliefs and ways of worship, yet they all have a common historical, cultural and civilizational legacy which binds them together emotionally; this common legacy is what is called Hindutva. Occasionally the term 'Hindu' is used loosely to describe all different faiths which have branched out from Hindu religion. In such contexts, the term "Hindu" should be understood in the sense of Hindutva, rather than as referring strictly to the Hindu religion.

Strength of Hindutva

Finally, Savarkar makes a prediction - 'Thirty crores of people,* with India for their basis of operation, for their fatherland and for their Holyland with such a history behind them, bound together by ties of a common blood and common culture can dictate their terms to the whole world. A day will come when mankind will have to face the force.

Equally certain it is that whenever the Hindus come to hold such a position whence they could dictate terms to the whole world, - those terms cannot be very different from the terms which Gita dictates or the Buddha lays down.'[7]

*The then population of Bharatvarsh.

Challenges for Hindus

To turn Savarkar's prophesy into reality, Hindus face several serious challenges which need to be elaborated. A society ignorant of challenges can't achieve great goals.

As discussed earlier, word 'Hindu religion' encompasses Sanatan, Dharma (duty) and religion (ways of worship). We have also discussed how Hindus differ from the followers of other religions (Islam and Christianity). A basic difference between these religions, especially Islam and Hindu religion is this: besides being a religion, Islam also has a political aspect viz. concept of an ideal state as the one governed as per Sharia (Islamic rule). Further, it is mandated for every Muslim to strive for spread of Islam and establishment of Islamic rule wherever it is not prevalent.

On the other hand, Hindus never had any political aspect to their religious beliefs. Hindus never believed in spreading their faith, least of all by force. Sarva Dharma Sambhav (equal respect for all religions) being their motto, where was the need to persuade others to convert to Hindu religion? Hindu Kings were expected to adhere to Raj dharma (duties of a ruler) which in essence meant ruling for the welfare of their subjects (*praja*) in an impartial manner.

The biggest challenge that 'Sarva Dharma Sambhav' believing Hindus have faced for centuries and face even today is how to reconcile with adherents of those religions which believe in their own supremacy and seek to impose their own beliefs on others.

Hindutva as a Bulwark Against Religious Extremism

Undoubtedly, aggressively assertive religious groups can pose a challenge to peaceful others as they constantly strive to impose their religious beliefs on them by any means, fair or foul.

In medieval times, peace loving Hindus could not stand up to the violence of the invaders, however, in the changed circumstances of present day, Hindus are not helpless anymore. From ancient times Hindus have had the power of mind and heart but less of muscle. Faced with the muscle power, they succumbed resulting in centuries of oppression. Today they must use their mind (intellect) to safeguard their present and future. Enumerated hereunder are some fundamental principles to ensure that Hindus never again face what they have had to face for centuries:

1. Proud to be a Hindu

As exhorted by Savarkar, Hindus should be conscious of the fact that they are inheritors of a great ancient culture and civilization and take pride in it. Once we are proud of something, we protect and defend it with all our might.

2. Zero Tolerance for Disrespect of Hindu Beliefs

While we follow the principle of Sarva Dharma Sambhav (equal respect for all religions), we expect followers of other religions to have similar attitude towards Hindus. It should be unambiguously understood that Hindus will not tolerate any disrespect towards any of their faiths, beliefs or practices and will respond forcefully and effectively in case of such disrespect from any quarter.

3. Hindus Must Unite Socially*

Hindu society is a deeply divided one, hence inherently weak. As against this, minorities (for example Muslims) are united, at least on religious issues. As we have already discussed, the most debilitating aspect of Hindu society has been the historical oppression of the weaker sections especially dalits by the upper castes. It is true that our constitution has made appropriate provisions for protection of oppressed classes; it is also an unfortunate reality that still some segments of upper castes continue to look down upon them. This is evident from the occasional reporting of harassment and targeting of dalits. Hindu society cannot be strong if a large segment of it is held in contempt and disdain. We do not have the option to let the Hindu society continue as weak as it is. We must strengthen the Hindu society overcoming the caste prejudices. We must recognise only one reality: we are Hindus first and Hindus last. Caste can continue to be our identity but not in the sense of superior or inferior. All Castes are equal; all are Hindus.

Gurudev Rabindranath Tagore on Need for Hindu Unity

It is pertinent to quote here what Gurudev Rabindranath Tagore felt about lack of Hindu unity. Tagore was concerned about the lack of unity among Hindus. In an article titled 'Swami Shraddananda' published in 'Kalanter' (collection of his essays), Tagore writes: 'When a Muslim called upon the Muslim community, he did not find any obstacle – he called in the name of one God……. And, today when we (Hindus) call 'come on, Hindus', who will respond? How many small communities, how many boundaries, how much provincialism divides us – who will come after overcoming these (differences)? How many dangers have we encountered; where did we come together? When Mohammed Ghouri brought the first blow from outside, the Hindus could not be united, even in the days of imminent danger. After that, when temples started being demolished one after another, and idols of Gods started being crushed, the Hindus fought and died in small units, but they could not be united. They were killed because they were divided, it has been proven time and again.'[9]

Gurudev's words are as relevant today as they were when they were written (1920s). If a person like Tagore, who is variously described as a humanist, universalist, internationalist is constrained to express such anguished views as above about Hindu disunity, we the Hindus must take note and unite, for our own sake.

4. Hindus Must Unite Politically*

In an electoral democracy like Bharatvarsh, a united minority group can command an influence disproportionate to its numbers. This disproportionate influence is much more aggravated if the majority is fragmented. Hence, Hindus must unite politically. Political unity implies not accepting disregard of their interests by various political parties. This implies boycotting pseudo secular parties which thrive on appeasement of minority groups for their vote banks, at the cost of Hindu interests. It will send a clear message to them that minority appeasement will not pay.

5. Reclaiming Our Lost Heritage – Restoration of Temples

It is an indisputable fact that during Muslim rule several Hindu Temples were destroyed and mosques constructed on their sites. Historical documents, some of them authored by contemporary Muslim writers are available as evidence. All such destroyed temples need to be restored after following due process. It should be done through mutual discussion between the communities, if possible. In case this option is not available, the matter should be pursued through courts of law.

It is worth mentioning that forcible change of character of places of worship did take place in other countries also apart from Bharatvarsh. Let's see what happened to such places of worship over time.

Spain was a Christian state which was captured by Muslims in 711 CE; it continued to be under Muslim rule for over 700 years. During this period several churches were converted into mosques. After restoration of Christian rule in 1492 CE, several such mosques were restored as churches. For example, the cathedral at Cordoba was converted into a mosque in the beginning of eighth century. However, after recapture of Cordoba by Christians, King Ferdinand III got the cathedral restored in 1236 CE.

Hagia Sophia church in Istanbul (Turkey) was constructed in 537 CE during Roman empire. After establishment of Ottoman empire, it was converted into a mosque in 1453 CE. In 1923 Turkey was declared as a republic. In 1935, Hagia Sophia was converted into a museum, however, in 2020 it was again declared a mosque.

Above examples are illustrative of the fact that with change of religious character of regime, change in the character of places of worship has been the rule rather than exception. Only difference is, in medieval times it was done by force, in the present it should be done through mutual discussions, if possible or through legal process.

Savarkar's Exhortation

Before we close this Chapter, let's read the exhortation of Savarkar to Hindus:

'The English and the Americans feel they are kith and kin because they possess a Shakespeare in common. But not only Kalidas or a Bhasa but, Oh Hindus! Ye possess a Ramayana and Mahabharat in common–and the Vedas! One of the national songs the American children are taught to sing attempts to rouse their sense of eternal self importance by pointing out to the hundred years twice told that stand behind their history. The Hindu counts his years not by centuries but by cycles–the Yuga and the Kalpa.......

'Besides culture the ties of common holy land has at times proved stronger than the chains of a Motherland. Look at the Mohammeddans. Mecca to them is a sterner reality than Delhi or Agra........ Look at the Jews; neither centuries of prosperity nor sense of gratitude for the shelter they found, can make them more attached or even equally attached to the several countries they inhabit. Their love is, and must necessarily be divided between the land of their birth and the land of their prophets. If the Zionists' dreams are ever realised–if Palestine becomes a Jewish state......... they, like the Mohammedans would naturally set the interests of their holy land above those of their motherland in America and Europe and in case of war between their adopted country and the Jewish state, would naturally sympathise with the latter, if indeed they do not bodily go over to it. History is too full of examples of such desertions to cite particulars. The crusades again, attest to the wonderful influence that a common holy land exercises over peoples widely separated in race, nationality and language, to bind and hold them together.'

'The ideal conditions, therefore, under which a nation can attain perfect solidarity and cohesion would, other things being equal, be found in the case of those people who inhabit the land they adore, the land of whose forefathers is also the land of their Gods and Angels, of Seers and Prophets; the scenes of whose history are also the scenes of their mythology.

The Hindus are about the only people who are blessed with these ideal conditions that are at the same time incentive to national solidarity, cohesion and greatness.'[8]

* These aspects are covered in more details in the next chapter.

Chapter-7

Imperative Need for Hindu Unity

We have touched upon the need for Hindu unity in earlier chapters, however, this matter is of such paramount importance as to deserve a fuller discussion in a separate chapter.

Were Hindus Weak?

Consider a well read intellectual say a scientist whose main occupation is exploring and solving the mysteries of the nature. Such a person is possessed of great power of mind. As he does not need the power of muscle to pursue his vocation, he did not care to develop the same. Then one day some neighbourhood goons forcibly enter his house and not only loot him, they thrash him physically. Not possessed of the muscle power to match that of the goons, he feels helpless to defend himself against them. What is true for individuals is true of societies and nations too. We have already discussed the nature of ancient Hindu society - progressive and intellectual with freedom of thought and belief, open to new ideas, belief in high moral values and ideals. We have also discussed nature of the invaders. Totally opposite to the Hindus - uncouth, bigoted, merciless, intolerant of any belief other than their own....... Bharatvarsh was a land where kings did fight wars to expand their kingdom, but even wars were fought adhering to a code of conduct which included ensuring minimal harm to the general populace. On the other hand, invaders had no compunction in killing and looting general population indiscriminately. In short, Hindus had more of brain power and relatively less of brawn power, whereas the invaders had only brawn power and were devoid of brain power. One more thing Hindus lacked in addition to the brawn power, and we have discussed this earlier - unity. The answer to the question, 'were Hindus weak' is yes, but not so much because of lesser brawn power (relative to the invaders), more so because of the lack of unity in the Hindu society especially on the basis of caste. It was a resounding demonstration of the aphorism 'United we stand, divided we fall'; we fell because we were divided.

Did We Learn Any Lessons?

None whatsoever. Another aphorism - 'Those who do not learn from past mistakes, are set to repeat them.' Hindus do not seem to have learnt any lessons from their past mistakes, as demonstrated by the events of past several centuries. As a detailed discussion on the history of Hindu's lack of unity is not feasible, we will restrict it to the period after the partition and independence of the country.

Hindu Society at Independence

At the time of independence, Hindu society was

deeply divided based on caste, language, regions etc. Most intractable of these divisions was the caste. As we have discussed earlier, oppression of lower castes by the upper castes played a significant part in the spread of Islam in Bharatvarsh. This factor alone should have induced introspection in the Hindu society, but that was not to be. Oppression of the lower castes (dalits) continued largely unabated. At Independence dalits were in a pitiable situation socially and economically. For sure, the constitution makers did make provisions in the Constitution for safeguarding and protecting the interests of Dalits, such as reservations in educational institutions and jobs and outlawing untouchability. Whereas issues of region and language were resolved, by and large satisfactorily by judicious reorganization of the States on linguistic basis, the matter of dalits' oppression was not that straightforward to resolve. Constitutional provisions did, over time, lead to higher representation of dalits in educational institutions and services. However, the mental block and prejudices which the higher castes have harboured for centuries, though somewhat mitigated over time, have not vanished totally. Even today, occasionally, there are news reports of harassment or even violence against dalits on mundane issues such as drawing water from village well.

Consequence of Lack of Hindu Unity

Before independence, British rulers under their divide

and rule policy made full use of divisions in the Hindu society to sustain their rule. After independence, that tried and tested formula (divide and rule) was adopted by the new rulers. Country was divided on communal lines. With creation of Pakistan, it was expected that bulk of muslims would migrate to that newly created nation for which they had fought vigorously and passionately. It was a dream come true for them. Why would any one of the Bharatvarsh's Muslims not go to live in a state governed as per Sharia rather than continue to live in a secular state? The fact remains that a vast majority of muslims did not migrate to Pakistan and it was mainly because of the labours of the leaders of the Congress party led by Mahatma Gandhi and Jawaharlal Nehru. There were several leaders who favoured exchange of population in view of the division of the country on communal basis, Dr B.R. Ambedkar being one of them. He wrote prophetically: 'It must be admitted that by the creation of Pakistan, Hindustan is not freed of the communal question. While Pakistan can be made a homogeneous state, Hindustan must remain a composite state. The only way to make Hindustan homogeneous is to arrange for exchange of population. Until that is done, it must be admitted that even with the creation of Pakistan, the problem of majority vs minority will remain in Hindustan as before and will continue to produce disharmony in the body politic of Hindustan.'[1]

Such leaders (who favoured exchange of population) were labeled as 'communal'. Naturally they were 'enemies' in the eyes of the Muslims and who were the friends? Congress leaders who facilitated their continued stay in Bharatvarsh. The seeds of selective secularism (pseudo secularism), appeasement and vote bank politics were sown immediately after independence. Question arises, why would a political party appease and woo a group comprising 10% (appx. population of muslims in Bharatvarsh after partition) and not the majority Hindus who comprised 84%. Answer is simple—the muslims of Bharatvarsh formed a united political block (vote bank) where as the Hindus were a divided lot—divided on the basis of language, region and caste. Winning formula perfected by the ruling party was formidable: appease the minority group by giving them preferential treatment, conceding even their unreasonable demands and look the other way to their misdemeanours, for their 'vote bank' and get votes of sections of Hindus appealing to language, regional and/or caste groups.

Further, they made every effort to suppress and downplay the only thread that emotionally bound the Hindus of all denominations for centuries viz. Sanatan. It was no coincidence that Jawaharlal Nehru abhorred the idea of 'Hindu revivalism' with no such abhorence for other religions. Such statements and sentiments against Hindu religion coming from top leaders naturally had a dampening and demoralizing effect on Hindus. Success of the 'vote bank' politics induced several other political parties to tread the same path. As a result, there is a plethora of 'pseudo secular' parties today.

Hindu Revivalism

Over 5000 years old civilization suppressed for centuries could not be kept down permanently; it had to assert itself one day and it did. Hindu community's struggle for restoration of Ram Janmbhoomi temple at Ayodhya became the catalyst for 'Hindu revivalism'. It can be stated without fear of contradiction that bulk of the Hindus who participated in the struggle belonged to the lower strata of Hindu society. Hindu society finally started to awaken from the deep slumber of centuries. The vehemence with which the pseudo secular parties and others (journalists, writers and historians) opposed restoration of the temple, exposed themselves in the eyes of many Hindus. Sensing that Hindus had begun to see through their game, they invented new devices to keep Hindus divided on caste basis. Earlier Hindus were mainly divided as dalits vs the rest. Now they created new fault lines between OBCs (other backward castes) and others by offering reservations to OBCs. Desirability or otherwise of such reservations is not relevant here, what is relevant is that new fault lines were created within the Hindu society to further fragment it. Parts of these fragments along with solid Muslim vote bank catapulted many 'pseudo secular' parties to power. This is how 'divide Hindus' and capture solid Muslim vote bank worked. As already mentioned, Muslim vote bank came at a price viz. appeasement - support for Muslim side in any dispute with Hindus (this explains pseudo secular's opposition to reconstruction of Ram Temple at Ayodhya), making laws to blatantly appease Muslims (law passed in the wake of Shahbano judgement of SC, Places of worship act and Waqf act) turning a blind eye to incidents of atrocities against Hindus (the forced exodus of Kashmiri Pandits, and incidents of riots or attacks on Hindu processions). It is of paramount importance to understand that this heavy price for support of Muslim vote bank to pseudo secular parties has been paid by the Hindus - disunited Hindus.

Imperativeness of Hindu Unity

Gist of the foregoing narrative is this: Hindus have paid very heavy price for disunity over centuries and are still paying. What should Hindus do? Obvious answer is that Hindus must unite. But unite in what way? Should Hindus come out on the streets in large numbers when ever attacked by the members of some other community? Yes that's one way of showing solidarity. However, let it be understood that Hindus just can't match organised violence by matching violence. Reason is obvious. Whereas for some, violence is part and parcel of their ideological upbringing, Hindus are taught the virtues of non-violence and compassion (most Hindus are loath to kill even ants, some even feed them wheat flour). Secondly, Hindus have only this land called Bharatvarsh as their mother land and meeting violence by violence will not be conducive to the overall interests of Bharatmata. Then, how do Hindus unite? Hindus must unite politically, the way Muslim community has united to form a vote bank. In medieval times it was 'brawn power' that prevailed over vast majority of Hindus, in the present times the 'numbers power' must prevail. Now that Hindus have understood the game of pseudo secular parties, they must end this game by rejecting such parties lock stock and barrel. They must send an unambiguous message to all political parties that appeasement of minorities at the cost of their (Hindus') interests and national interest will not be tolerated. Hindus must vote for parties which, if not pro-hindu are at least genuinely secular; parties which will not sacrifice Hindu and national interests at the alter of appeasement for the sake of power. A truly secular party is one whose actions are religion neutral. Who will not pass laws to favour a particular minority community (or against hindu interests); who will not compromise with national security to please a particular community; who will not proclaim that the first right on national resources is that of a particular community; who will not stand in the way of Hindus right to claim their destroyed haritage through legal action; who will recognise, respect and nurture 5000 years Hindu civilization (as against Hindu religion which Hindus are capable of looking after themselves) and not try to equate it with alien cultures in the name of secularism.

It is unrealistic to expect that Hindus can forget their inherent differences of language, region and caste which have defined their identities for thousands of years. But it is not unrealistic to expect Hindus to place their Hindu identity above all other identities, because their identities of language, region and caste survive as long as their Hindu identity survives. While retaining and being proud of their various identities, Hindus must give up the mindset that their own identity especially of caste is superior to others. No caste is superior or inferior, all are equal, all are Hindus.

Once the message of Hindu unity (consolidation) against pseudo secularism and appeasement is understood by political parties, they will be forced to change or perish. New parties will come into existence. Let there be any number of political parties, professing different socio-economic policies but with one common feature viz. all truly secular in the sense defined above. No appeasement of any community. No compromise with national interests to please any community.

CHAPTER-8

Sanatan, Hindu Religion and Secularism

What is Secularism? Is Bharatvarsh a Secular State?

Secularism is essentially a western concept, according to which, the State should be governed based on policies and principles which are uninfluenced by any religion. Under the constitution of a secular State, all citizens, irrespective of the faiths they profess, should be treated as equals and should have equal rights. The concept of secularism is relevant for societies in which the dominant religion has a sense of superiority over other religions. In such societies, those professing minority religions tend to develop a sense of being discriminated against, giving rise to demand to keep religion out of governance and let the religion be in the personal domain of each individual. Sanatan with the moto 'Sarva Dharma Sambhav' (equal respect for all religions) is the epitome of secularism; if all religions are to be respected equally, where is the question of discrimination against anyone?

Our constitution is presumed to be based upon secular principles. In a constitution based upon the western definition of secularism, it's provisions should have nothing to do with any religion. All provisions should apply equally to all citizens, irrespective of their religion. There should be no mention of terms such as 'majority' or 'minority' in such a constitution. These terms divide the society based on religion, hence are inconsistent with the concept of secularism and equality.

Now let's consider some of the features of our constitution.

Article 14. Equality before Law

The State shall not deny to any person equality before the law or the equal protection of the laws within the territory of India.

Article 19

This Article grants following rights to all citizens (with some conditions):

* to freedom of speech and expression;

* to assemble peaceably and without arms;

* to form associations or unions or co-operative societies;

* to move freely throughout the territory of India;

* to reside and settle in any part of the territory of India; and

* to practise any profession, or to carry on any occupation, trade or business.

Article 21. Protection of Life and Personal Liberty
No person shall be deprived of his life or personal liberty except according to procedure established by law.

It is noteworthy that in none of these Articles, terms 'minority' or 'majority' have been mentioned, instead terms 'citizens' and 'persons' have been mentioned. Rightly so, because the rights enshrined in these Articles are available to all citizens including minorities. Hence, these Articles are consistent with the definition of secularism. Let us consider some more Articles.

Article 29. Protection of Interests of Minorities
(1) Any section of the citizens residing in the territory of India or any part thereof having a distinct language, script or culture of its own shall have the right to conserve the same.

(2) No citizen shall be denied admission into any educational institution maintained by the State or receiving aid out of State funds on grounds only of religion, race, caste, language or any of them.

Article 30. Right of Minorities to Establish and Administer Educational Institutions
(1) All minorities, whether based on religion or language, shall have the right to establish and administer educational institutions of their choice.

(1A) In making any law providing for the compulsory acquisition of any property of an educational institution established and administered by a minority, referred to in clause (1), the State shall ensure that the amount fixed by or determined under such law for the acquisition of such property is such as would not restrict or abrogate the right guaranteed under that clause.

(2) The state shall not, in granting aid to educational institutions, discriminate against any educational institution on the ground that it is under the management of a minority, whether based on religion or language.

Question arises, are the rights under Articles 29 and 30 available to majority community? If yes, then these Articles are superfluous, if not then the constitution discriminates against the majority community, granting additional rights to minorities, in contravention to the principle of secularism.

Some well-meaning persons can argue that in absence of these provisions, the possibility of discrimination against the minorities would be there. However, that possibility remains despite Articles 29 and 30. If a person from a minority community is denied admission to an educational institution, they can seek redressal by approaching a court of law under Article 29. In absence of Article 29 also, the option to seek redressal would still be available under

Article 14 (equality before law) which does not allow discrimination on any ground including religion.

Further, there are several financial assistance packages such as scholarships, loans etc., especially for minorities. Then there are minority educational institutions (Aligarh Muslim University, Jamia Millia Islamia) funded by the government. How does all this reconcile with the definition of secularism viz. State policies should be totally devoid of the religious considerations?

Contravention of the principles of secularism began soon after implementation of the constitution on January 26, 1950, in the form of Hindu Code Bills (set of 4 legislations codifying and reforming the Hindu personal laws relating to marriage, succession, guardianship and adoption). A law bearing the word 'Hindu' in a secular constitution! Strange indeed. But then the anachronistic Hindu personal laws needed to be reformed. So were the Muslim personal laws in the need of reforms. Right course would have been to introduce religion neutral Uniform Civil Code (UCC), without reference to any religion, with a provision that in case of any conflict between the personal law and the UCC, the latter shall prevail. This course would have been consistent with the principles of secularism. Why then this course was not followed? Therein lies the genesis of 'pseudo secularism'.

George Orwell's famous novel Animal Farm has a much-quoted sentence – 'All animals (residing in the Animal Farm) are equal but some are more equal than others'. Had the constitution not had Articles 29 and 30, the moto of our constitution would have been – 'All citizens are equal'. However, with these Articles the moto is – 'All citizens are equal, but minorities are more equal than majority.'

From the above discussion we can easily conclude if Bharatvarsh is a truly secular State.

Secularism as a Political Tool

As discussed above, our constitution and some of the laws framed under it are not consistent with the definition of secularism. Then, what do our politicians imply when they swear by secularism? Their secularism is exactly opposite to what it ought to be. For them, secularism means appeasement of minorities to garner their votes. For want of a better term to describe their kind of 'secularism', a term 'pseudo secularism' has been coined. We can define a pseudo secular politician (or political party) as the one *who indulges in appeasement of minorities, for their votes, even at the cost of interests of the majority or the larger interests of the country.*

This definition is incomplete unless we define the term 'appeasement'. As per Collins Dictionary 'Appeasement means giving people what they want to prevent them from harming you or being angry with you.' In the context of the politicians practicing pseudo secularism, we can define appeasement as *the practice of pandering to the demands of the minorities, justified or unjustified, with the objective of cultivating them as a vote bank*. In this definition, the key word is 'unjustified' because there can be no objection to acceding to the justified demands of anybody including minorities; what distinguishes pseudo seculars is their propensity to accede to even their unjustified demands. From the above discussion one may be led to believe that pseudo seculars are found amongst politicians only. It is not so. There exist pseudo secular writers, journalists, historians, economists etc. (so called intellectuals). The pseudo secularism of this class manifests itself as follows:

* Supporting all kinds of demands of minorities, justified or unjustified,

* Turning a blind eye to improper actions of minorities, even those against country's interests,

*Denying or rationalizing the atrocities, injustices, indignities suffered by Hindus during Islamic rule (including destruction of temples),

* Commenting adversely upon supposedly negative features of Sanatan/Hindu religion but refraining from doing so in respect of other religions.

In a nutshell they display a distinct anti Hindu and pro minorities bias. Significantly, all of them are Hindus themselves.

Question arises - politicians practice pseudo secularism for vote bank of minorities, why do these so-called intellectuals do so? Only they can provide the answer.

Is Hindu Rashtra Consistent with Secularism?

There is no conflict between the fundamental principles of Sanatan, Hindu religion, Hindu Rashtra and secularism. The moto 'Sarva Dharma Sambhav' (equal respect for all religions) of Sanatan is a resounding declaration of secularism. As already noted, need for the western concept of secularism arose in those societies in which the dominant religionists had a sense of superiority for themselves and inferiority for others. This naturally made minorities apprehensive and insecure, whence arose the need for separation of governance from religious considerations (secularism). With 'Sarva Dharm Sambhav' as the guiding moto, Sanatan itself is embodiment of secularism.

Chapter-9

British Raj and Bharatvarsh

After 600 years of Muslim rule, Bharatvarsh was destined to be ruled by another set of 'invaders' who did not come riding horses but ships. This class of 'invaders' included British, French, Dutch and Portuguese. Eventually the British outsmarted the others and took control of the destiny of Bharatvarsh for two centuries. They came as traders (East India Company) and in due course became its rulers (British Raj). We have already discussed the adversities suffered by Bharatvarsh in general and Hindus in particular during the Muslim rule. It is necessary to discuss the consequences of the British Raj, whose impact on Bharatvarsh has been no less detrimental.

A person can be proud of their wealth, knowledge, achievements, great ancestry etc. Same factors can be the reasons for the pride of a society or nation. Pride of a person can be destroyed thus:

* If reason for pride is wealth, depriving them of it,

* Convincing a person proud of their knowledge that their knowledge is, in fact, false,

* Someone proud of achievements can be convinced that their achievements are in fact insignificant, and others have achieved much more,

* The one proud of great ancestry can be put down by belittling their ancestors and abusing them.

Above stratagems can also be employed to destroy the pride of a people; Muslim rulers did exactly that with Hindus. As we will now see, British also used the same strategies with Bharatvarsh albeit with a difference. They were shrewder and more sophisticated than Muslim invaders. What Muslim rulers did crudely and brazenly, British did gradually, in a planned way. We will now discuss the damage caused to the people of Bharatvarsh by the British.

Bharatvarsh Before Arrival of British and Others

It is an established fact that before arrival of British and other Europeans, Bharatvarsh was one of the top world economies. As per one study,[1] Bharatvarsh's gross domestic product (GDP) in the year 1500 was second only to China and in the year 1700 it was the highest (with China being second).

Bharatvarsh was a major exporter of goods - food stuff (sugar, rice) and textiles. 'As an English agent observed, 'From Aden to Achin from head to foot, everyone was clothed in Indian textiles'. This statement, even though a little exaggerated ...... was essentially true. It was this which made India the virtual manufactory of the Asian world (excluding China).'[2]

Arrival of British

British East India Company's initial objective was

trading with east and south Asian countries including Bharatvarsh. It was incorporated by royal charter on December 31, 1600. They first arrived in Bharatvarsh in 1608. Starting as traders, the Company in due course got involved in politics. They raised an army and used it to annex territories. They exploited the local population by plundering wealth through heavy, unfair taxation and other coercive policies. Let's see briefly how East India Company and later British government reduced Bharatvarsh from a wealthy to a poor nation.

Agricultural and Rural Economy

For centuries, agriculture has contributed significantly to Bharatvarsh's economy. Accordingly, to destroy it economically and to break its moral they employed following methods:

* Imposed heavy land tax (lagaan) on the agricultural land, quantum of which had no relationship with the actual income derived from the land. The farmer had to compulsorily pay it even if, in any year, the crop failed due to any reason, say deficient rains. Quite often the farmers had to sell off their family gold and silver. Thereafter, they resorted to borrowing from money lenders at very high interest rates, for land tax had to be paid year after year, without respite. Most small farmers were never able to repay the debt and were in perpetual throes of debt and penury.

* For centuries, the main produce of Bharatvarsh's farmers had been food grains (wheat, rice, millet etc.). On the one hand these items fetched higher profits for the grower, on the other, it ensured buffer stocks of food grains which prevented hardships in times of draught. British forced them to shift to cash crops such as tea, sugar, coffee, opium, indigo. They would buy these items from farmers cheap and earn huge profits through exports. This policy not only pushed farmers further into poverty, but it also created shortages of food grains resulting in mass starvation and deaths in times of draughts.

In this context it is pertinent to recall forced cultivation of indigo in Bengal. In Britain indigo was used for dyeing of cloth and there was huge demand for it. British coerced farmers in Bengal to cultivate indigo instead of traditional food grains. Those who resisted were treated harshly, even whipped. British procured the produce from the farmers at a fraction of the market price and made huge profits by exporting it to Britain.

*Investments made by the British, over 200 years, for construction of irrigation canals etc. was not adequate for a country of Bharatvarsh's size. As such, in the event of inadequate rains, draughts were common with disastrous consequences. Some of the major draughts which caused wide spread havoc: Bengal (1770), Agra (1837), Orissa (1866), Bihar (1873), Daccan (1876),

Country wide draught (1896), Bombay (1905), Bengal (1943). Apart from these major draughts, in which millions perished, occurrence of localized draughts was a regular feature.

1943 Bengal draught in which more than three million perished due to hunger, needs special mention. World War second was at its peak. At the instance of Winston Churchill, the British Prime Minister, Indian resources including food grains were diverted for war efforts leaving hungry masses of Bengal in the lurch. No wonder, millions of hungry Bengalis perished.

Industries

For the economic progress of any country, it's industries must develop. Industrial growth makes it self-reliant and leads to creation of jobs, which in turn results in spread of prosperity among the masses. Conversely, to destroy its economy, it is sufficient to stymie its industrial growth. British did exactly that with Bharatvarsh. They had two-fold objective viz. to make it economically weak and to enrich Britain at its cost, which they accomplished successfully through their policies, such as follows:

*Imposition of heavy import duties on goods exported to Britain and duty free (or with nominal duties) imports from Britain.

*Importing raw material from Bharatvarsh and exporting back finished goods. This particularly impacted textile industry. British imported raw cotton, indigo etc. from Bharatvarsh and flooded it with cheap machine-made cotton. Consequently, the traditional handloom industry declined resulting in widespread unemployment and poverty.

*British did not encourage development of science and technology in Bharatvarsh. They did establish several universities, however, their objective for doing so was not to produce scientists and technologists; it was to create a pool of educated locals to assist them in running the administration. This was necessary as importing manpower from Britain in as large numbers as required to govern a country of Bharatvarsh's size was not feasible.

Let's now discuss how the British education policies profoundly impacted the cultural ethos of Bharatvarsh.

Education System

In respect of education system, adversities faced by Hindus during British rule were no less than those faced during Muslim rule. Muslim rulers were generally indifferent to the educational needs of Hindus. They set up madrasas and maktabs where Islamic education was imparted. For their children, Hindus continued to set up their own educational institutions such as pathshalas and gurukuls where education was imparted in Sanskrit and other local languages. Apart from the Sanskrit language, they were taught Hindu religious scriptures, mathematics, astronomy, astrology, philosophy, ethics, Ayurveda, yoga, meditation etc. Accordingly, Hindus were very much grounded in their culture and civilization. This changed drastically under the British.

In a 1835 policy paper known as 'Minute on Indian Education', Lord Babington Macaulay, made some far reaching recommendations to the Governor General Lord William Bentinck which drastically and profoundly changed the people of Bharatvarsh in more ways than one viz. how they dressed, talked, ate, spoke and even the way they thought. Let's have a look at some of his recommendations:

*English should replace the local languages as medium of instruction in schools.

*Traditional education should be discouraged.

*Publishing of books in Sanskrit and Arabic to be discouraged.

*Grants should be given for teaching western subjects.

*European literature and science to be promoted.

Macaulay's reasoning was based upon the following assumptions:

*Indian system of learning was inferior to European system.

*English was necessary for modern education.

* English education would create a class of locals who would be close to the ruling class in language, dress, culture and values. Macaulay believed (rightly) that this would ensure strengthening of British rule in Bharatvarsh.

Because of Macaulay's recommendations, pathshalas and gurukuls declined and eventually vanished. Hindus in general became admirers of English education, values, mannerism etc. Significantly, even today there are thousands of madrasas, whereas there may hardly be any gurukuls left.

Mother Tongue vs English

As noted above, because of British policies, Bharatvarsh's traditional education systems were replaced by western education. Additionally, importance of English language kept going up at the cost of indigenous languages. It is an established fact that the primary education of children is best done in their mother tongues. Reason is obvious. Children are naturally conversant with their mother tongues, hence can absorb knowledge more readily if taught in it rather than in English. However, today well to do sections of the society prefer to educate their children in English medium rather than mother tongue. The craze for English medium is now spreading even among the lower strata resulting in mushrooming of numerous so called English medium schools.

These days children of middle and upper classes are frequently seen conversing in English rather than in their mother tongues. Nothing could be more unfortunate than this.

Another fallout of primacy of English is the unfair advantage English speakers have over those who are not able to converse in English fluently but are no less qualified otherwise. It is a gross injustice to the true sons and daughters of the soil

It is not the case that English language has not benefitted us in any way. Since most books and literature on science, technology, medicine and several other subjects are in English, proficiency in the language has made all that knowledge available to us. Additionally, knowledge of English is an asset for someone desirous of acquiring higher education abroad.

Question arises, if English has benefitted us in so many ways, then what is the issue? Learning any language - English or any other is not the issue; the issue is giving primacy to the other language over the mother tongue. Children should learn English as a subject, but the medium of instruction (up to a certain level) should mandatorily be the mother tongue. Mother tongue is one of our three mothers (other two being the mother who gave birth and the mother land), hence we must respect it and should be proud of it.

Dress and Social Behaviour

One of the objectives of Macaulay was to make us 'English' in thought and behaviour (in other words make us anglicised slaves) and he has succeeded in this objective splendidly. Now the dresses our men wear are totally westernised. Even the women's dresses are being increasingly influenced by the west.

Western influence can be seen in day-to-day social behaviour and lifestyle of well to do segments of our society. Unfortunately, many such persons tend to look at everything our own, be it the country, city, religion, customs, beliefs etc. through the western-coloured glasses and under rate them vis-a-vis the west.

Give the Devil its Due

Even the most adverse events do have some unexpected positive aspects, and the British rule was no exception. Following can be considered as positive outcomes of the British rule:

*Political integration - Before arrival of the British, Bharatvarsh was a landmass comprising numerous small and big independent regions ruled by various chieftains (rajas, nawabs, sultans, jagirdars etc.). Each one of them had its own system of governance and laws. The British by use of force or through other devices captured many of those territories and integrated them into a single political entity - British India and introduced uniform governance and laws.

Although they did it for their own convenience, in the long run political integration of a major part of the country turned out to be a blessing in disguise.

*Introduction of new technology in infrastructure - Post industrial revolution, rapid technological developments were taking place in Europe. British brought many of those technologies such as railways, telegraph, airways to Bharatvarsh. They did so for their own needs of faster movement of personnel and goods. However, the infrastructure once created remained in place and eventually benefited the common people.

*Security against external threats - As part of the empire, British defended Bharatvarsh against external threats. It is inconceivable how Bharatvarsh would have been defended in the state in which it was when the British arrived.

As we can see from the above discussion, British rule was a mixed bag for the people of Bharatvarsh. Whether overall, it was beneficial or detrimental can be debated. However, on one point there is no doubt or dispute - British did plunder and impoverish the people of Bharatvarsh. As already noted earlier, when British arrived, Bharatvarsh was one of the wealthiest countries in the world and among the poorest when they left.

Muslim Rule vs British Rule

After 600 years of Muslim and 200 years of British

rule, it is remarkable that while Hindus carry a sense of outrage at the atrocities heaped upon their ancestors during the Muslim rule, no such sense of outrage exists in the minds of people against the British. Why? Possible reason could be as follows:

Muslim invaders and later rulers, in addition to plundering, killing and dishonouring (the women folk), struck at the very faith of Hindus by desecration and destruction of the symbols of their religion, culture and civilization. On the other hand, British did everything within their powers to enrich themselves at the cost of people of Bharatvarsh which, as we have discussed, led to their impoverishment. However, by and large, they refrained from doing anything which would hurt the honour and religious sentiments of the people.

It is an established fact that people do come to terms with losses of physical assets (money and property) with passage of time but assault on honour and faith create deep scars on the psychology of a person which just don't heal with time. What holds good for an individual, holds good for a society. Collective Hindu psyche may forget the financial hardships faced by their ancestors during Muslim and British rules by way of looting and plundering. However, the assault on their honour and faith inflicted by invaders and later Muslim rulers won't be, in fact can't be forgotten.

Chapter-10

Culture vs Religion

One fundamental difference between Hindus and followers of other religions, especially Muslims and Christians is this - whereas Hindus differentiate between culture and religion, followers of these religious do not. Bharatvarsh's Muslims and Christians believe that with conversion to another religion, their connection with Bharatvarsh's 5000 years old culture and civilization has also snapped. One reason for this attitude could the fact that most Muslims and Christians in Bharatvarsh are erstwhile Hindu dalits, who converted because of the discrimination and oppression faced by them. As such, they have a sense of revulsion towards anything related to Hindus, even culture and civilization. Be it as it may, today's Muslims and Christians should differentiate between method of worship (religion) and culture/civilization. As stated earlier, Hindus do understand this difference very well. On Christmas, many Hindus instal Christmas trees and light up their homes. Do they cease to be Hindus and instead become Christians? Not at all, because they do not go to church and attend the Christmas mass. Going to church is the religious aspect of Christmas and Christmas tree, lighting, cake etc. are cultural aspects. Similarly, Laxmi pujan on deepavali is religious aspect, bursting of crackers etc. is its cultural aspect. How many Muslims or Christians would burst crackers on deepavali?

In addition to their ability to differentiate between religion and culture, Hindus also believe that some principles and precepts are universal in nature; they are above religions, good for all humanity. Jesus Christ's message of love, compassion and forgiveness has a universal appeal. Who can be opposed to it? Hindus don't. So much so, numerous Hindus visit churches as tourists without any reservation and many light candles there as a mark of respect.

There are numerous messages of universal appeal in Hindu tradition. Whole life of Sri Ram is an example of how to discharge one's duty as a son, as a husband, as a brother, as a friend, duty towards the lowest strata of society and duty as a ruler. Significantly, none of these duties have anything to do with Hindu religion. All these duties are universal in nature. Should a Muslim or a Christian not discharge his/her duties say as a son, as a husband or as a friend?

In Bhagvat Gita, there could be some aspects which are not consistent with the basic tenets of other religions say the principle of rebirth. However, there is much in Gita which is of universal appeal. For example, how could anybody find fault with the exhortation of Sri

Krishna to concentrate on doing your duties (*karma*) without worrying about the outcome.

The point of the above discussion is this - religious minorities can embrace much from the ancient culture and civilization of Bharatvarsh, without in any way compromising with the tenets of their religions. They need to appreciate that with conversion, only the ways of worship (*puja padhyati*) changes; their connection with the ancient culture and civilization does not snap instantly. Much remains, with which they can continue to feel connected with, while practicing their new religion. For ages, Hindus have had the wisdom and broadness of vision to embrace the universal good irrespective of the source. Can the minorities display the same spirit? That's the million-dollar question.

Chapter-11

In a Nutshell

In the previous chapters we have discussed, in some details, subjects such as Sanatan, Hindu religion, Hindutva, Hindu Rashtra, secularism etc. We have also discussed some of the drawbacks and aberrations of Hindu society which to a large extent were responsible for long periods of subjugation and humiliation for Hindus. We mentioned some measures and precautions which Hindus must adopt so that history did not repeat itself. Let's review and consolidate all the points once again.

1. Hindus should be made aware of their glorious past

We Hindus should be proud of our ancient culture, civilisation and religion. However, this can happen only if Hindus are aware about it, and that too from the childhood. For this purpose, school curricula should include topics highlighting the glory of ancient Bharatvarsh, in various fields of human endeavour such as spirituality, ethics, art and architecture, sciences, public administration, economics etc. Given the limitations of secularism, it may not be possible to impart such knowledge in government schools. Hence, it must be done in families and private educational institutions. High standard books on

Sanatan culture and civilisation should be written by scholars in various Indian languages catering to different age groups, especially children.

2. Respect and be proud of the mother tongue

As mother tongue is an integral part of our culture and civilization, we can't be proud of the later without being proud of the former. Nowadays, children of well to do families are often seen conversing in English rather than their mother tongues. Quite a few of Hindi speaking children can't read Hindi texts and don't even know Hindi terms for numbers. This is a most unfortunate situation and needs to be corrected if we want our future generations to be proud of Bharatvarsh's ancient culture and civilization. This situation has come about due the propensity of the well to do (and not so well to do also) to educate their children in English medium schools. Some may argue that such English medium educated form a miniscule segment of the society and for vast masses medium of education is the mother tongue. This miniscule segment is looked upon by the rest as the role model. Even parents of modest means yearn to have their children educated in English medium and would go extra mile, sometimes beyond their means to do so. Another reason for this craze for education in English medium is the unfair advantage enjoyed by those who speak English fluently, over others who are not as proficient in the language but may be more qualified in all other respects.

As noted earlier, even otherwise, mother tongue is better suited for imparting education more effectively, at least in initial years.

Imparting education in mother tongue affords following advantages:

i) ensures imparting of education more effectively, especially in early years,

ii) ensures level playing field to all irrespective of the medium of education,

iii) fosters a sense of pride in the mother tongue without which one can't be proud of one's cultural and civilizational heritage.

The above situation can be brought about by the government, by making the local language as the medium of instructions compulsory up to class 8 in all schools, government or private. Can government make such a stipulation? If government can make rules such as minimum and maximum age for admission to schools, subjects and syllabus to be taught, conduct of examinations etc., it can certainly make another rule making it mandatory to have medium of education as Indian languages. Off course English should be taught as a subject.

3. Bharatvarsh is a Hindu Rashtra

Bharat, the country is governed by the constitution and Bharatvarsh, the Hindu Rashtra (nation) follows the customs and traditions of Sanatan culture and civilisation.

4. Hindus respect all religions and expect 'others' to respect them

Respect for all religions is the basic tenet of Sanatan (Sarva Dharma Sambhav). Hindus believe in this principle and expect followers of other religions to show similar respect toward the religious sentiments of Hindus. Hindus must not countenance any disrespect towards their religion, beliefs and sentiments by anyone. In the event of that happening, Hindus must protest strongly and effectively.

5. Need for strong and effective Hindu organisations

There is need for strong Hindu organisations to take lead in organising and uniting Hindus. They should conduct campaigns through public contact, social media etc. to educate Hindus about Sanatan, Hindu Rashtra, Hindutva etc. This will help create a sense of pride amongst Hindus towards their ancient culture and civilisation. In addition, these Hindu organisations should organise and lead protests against atrocities suffered by Hindus and/or disrespect towards Sanatan.

6. Hindus must rise above caste and unite

Hindus must rise above considerations of Caste and follow the principle - Hindu first, Caste second. No Caste is higher or lower, all Castes are equal, all are Hindus. As already discussed, division on Caste basis has caused immense damage to the Hindu society and Bharatvarsh, whose aftermath we are facing even to this day.

7. No special rights and privileges for non-hindus

Sanatan's Sarva Dharma Sambhav is the true definition of secularism. Provisions of our constitution granting equal rights to all citizens are consistent with the principles of secularism. However, some provisions which grant special rights to the minorities are in violation. As such, either those rights be granted to Hindus as well or such provisions should be abolished.

8. Boycott pseudo secular political parties

Some political parties have played the game of appeasement of some specific minorities shamelessly, unmindful of the national interests and/or interests of Hindus. Hindus should boycott such political parties. Let a message go to them that consolidation of specific minorities vote banks will be more than offset by counter consolidation of Hindus against them.

9. Restore temples destroyed in the past

There are several mosques which are said to have been constructed during Muslim rule after demolition of temples. All such cases should be surveyed by government agencies (Archaeological Survey of India). In case it is established without any doubt that a temple pre-existed at the site of a particular mosque, the mosque should be shifted to another site and temple restored. This should be done preferably through dialogue between the two communities, failing which legal process should be followed.

REFERENCES

Chapter 2: Sanatan/Hindu Culture & Civilization

1. *The Wonder That Was India*, A.L Basham, Rupa & Co, 1995 edition, pp. 350.
2. *Vastu-Sastra Vol. I Hindu Science of Architecture*, D.N.Shukla, Professor and Head of Dept. of Sanskrit, Punjab University, Chandigarh, 1961, pp. 90-91.
3. *Unesco World Heritage Convention – Ajanta Caves* (https://whc.unesco.org/en/list/242/).
4. *Unesco World Heritage Convention – Ellora Caves* (https://whc.unesco.org/en/list/243/).
5. *Wikipedia – Ellora Caves*
6. *Indian Culture (Government of India) – Kailasa: The Majestic Temple of Ellora*
   (https://indianculture.gov.in/stories/kailasa-majestic-temple-ellora).
7. *Mahabharat, Shanti Parva*, Gita Press, Gorakhpur, pp. 4561-4569.
8. War in Ancient India, V.R. Ramachandra Dikshitar, MacMillan and Co, 1944), pp 61
9. Ibid, pp 62
10. Ibid, 67-75
11. Ibid, pp 71
12. Ibid, pp 87
13. Ibid, pp 88
14. The Wonder That Was India, A.L Basham, Rupa & Co, 1995 edition, pp 9
15. Ibid, pp 498
16. History of Science and Technology in ancient India – The Beginnings (A project sponsored by National Institute of Science Technology & Development Studies, Published by Firma KLM Pvt Ltd., Calcutta, 1986], pp 113

17. Ibid, pp 122
18. Sulba Sutra - A critical Analysis, K Jayashankara, A thesis submitted to the Mangalore University for Degree of Doctor of Philosophy in Sanskrit, February 2007, pp 30
19. History of Science and Technology in ancient India – The Beginnings (A project sponsored by National Institute of Science Technology & Development Studies, Published by Firma KLM Pvt Ltd., Calcutta, 1986], pp 159-160
20. Ibid, pp 462
21. Aryabhatiya of Aryabhata, Kripa Shankar Shukla and KV Sarma, Indian National Science Academy, New Delhi, 1976 edition, pp xvii – xx
22. Ibid, Ganit Pad, pp 38-39, verse 6 (a-b)
23. Ibid, Ganit Pad, pp 40, verse 7 (a-b)
24. Ibid, Ganit Pad, pp 40-41, verse 7(c-d)
25. Ibid, Ganit Pad, pp 42
26. Ibid, Ganit Pad, pp 45 Circumference Diameter ratio - verse 10
27. Ibid, Ganit Pad, pp 70, verse 27(c-d)
28. Ibid, Ganit Pad, pp 73-74, verse 31
29. Ibid, Gola Pad, pp 119, verse 9
30. Ibid, Gola Pad, pp 151, verse 38
31. https://riskavoider.com/pythagoras-indigenous-knowledge/
32. Kautilya's Arthashastra, Government Press, Bangalore, 1915 Translated into English by R.Samasatry, pp 362
33. Ibid, pp 50-52
34. Ibid, pp 36-40
35. Ibid, pp 77-80
36. Ibid, pp 81-86
37. Ibid, pp 91-94
38. Ibid, pp 213-218
39. Ibid, pp 317-319
40. Ibid, pp 218-230

41. Ibid, pp 326
42. Ibid, pp 434

Chapter 3: Hindu Religion/Society - Strengths, Aberrations & Misconceptions

1. The Wonder That Was India, A.L.Basham, Rupa & Co.), pp 180

Chapter 4: Hindus vs Followers of Other Religions

1. Ancient India, DN Jha, Manohar Publishers, 2009 edition, pp 124, 125
2. The Wonder That was India, A.L.Basham, 1967 edition, pp 61
3. Historical Study of The Arrival of Apostle St. Thomas in Kerala and Its Influence on The Life of the St. Thomas Christians (Executive Summery) by Fr. Dr. Thomson Robi, Deptt of History, Baselius College, Kottayam, Kerala, September 2016
4. An Advanced History of India, RC Majumdar, HC Raychaudhuri, Kalikinkar Datta, Fourth Edition, McMillan India Ltd., pp 173, 174
5. Ibid, pp 270
6. Pakistan or The Partition of India, Dr. B.R.Ambedkar, Thacker & Co., Third Edition 1946 (Govt. of Maharashtra's First Edition, January 1990), pp 55
7. Ibid, pp 56
8. Ibid, pp 57
9. Ibid, pp 60
10. Ibid, pp 62-63
11. Muslim Separatism – Causes and Consequences, Sita Ram Goel, Voice of India, Chapter III
12. Wikipedia https://en.wikipedia.org/wiki/Aurangzeb [Reference: Truschke, Audrey (2017). Aurangzeb: The Life and Legacy of India's Most Controversial King, Stanford University Press. p. 56]
13. Jizyah, Harsh Narayan, Voice of India, Chapter 3 (Jizyah in India)

Chapter 6: Hindu Religion and Hindutva

1. Hindutva – Who is a Hindu?, Vinayak Damodar Savarkar, Veer Savarkar Prakashan, Savarkar Sadan, Mumbai, Fifth Edition (1969), pp 82
2. Ibid, pp 89-90
3. Ibid, pp 100-101
4. Ibid, pp 118-119
5. Ibid, pp 121
6. Ibid, pp 125
7. Ibid, pp 141
8. Ibid, pp 134-136
9. https://tagoreweb.in/Essays/kalantar-135

Chapter 7: Imperative of Hindu unity

1. Pakistan or The Partition of India, Dr. B.R.Ambedkar, Thacker & Co., Third Edition 1946 (Govt. of Maharashtra's First Edition, January 1990), pp 117

Chapter 9: British Raj and Bharatvarsh

1. 500 years of GDP: A tale of two countries - Article by Wendell Cox in newgeography dated 21/9/2015

   (https://www.newgeography.com/content/005050-500-years-gdp-a-tale-two-countries)
2. A History of Medieval India (800 - 1700), Satish Chandra, Orient BlackSwan, 2014 edition, pp 312